HEAVENMOVES

STEPHANIE BARRERA

HEAVEN MOVES by Stephanie Barrera.

All rights reserved. Printed in the United States of America. No part of this book may be used or reproduced in any manner whatsoever without written permission except in the case of brief quotations embodied in critical articles or reviews, except as provided by the United States of America copyright law.

Copyright © 2017

For information contact: 405 SW 148th Ave.
                              Davie, FL 33325
                              stephaniemarielive@gmail.com

Book and Cover design by Stephanie Barrera

First Edition: June 2017

There are a few key women in my life that taught me, challenged me, or re-inspired me to dance. This book is dedicated to you. Thank you for never giving up on me and for reminding me I was made to move.

CONTENTS

Foreward 1

Introduction 3

Section One: Dance and Heaven 5

Section Two : Dance on Earth 41

1: Alignment and Engagement 43

2: Warm Yet? 61

3: "Technically…" 67

4: Elasti-Girl 73

5: Conditioning 81

6: Nutrition and Body Care 89

Section Three: On Earth as in Heaven 99

Journal 109

FOREWARD

Never had I thought that at 24 years of age I would be writing a book, but here I am; a living testimony that God fulfills dreams and that His timing is perfect. The partnership I have undergone with the Lord has been the most interesting part of this journey, as I have understood that we can colabor and cocreate dreams with Jesus and He enjoys it as much or even more than we do. The journey to writing this book all began as I sat eating dinner with my parents two years ago one night in West Palm Beach. My father suggested that after I graduate with my Bachelors in Dance Pedagogy I take a year to establish a dance training program in Colombia and in some churches we were connected with, since he pastored them. I felt Holy Spirit telling me to listen to my dad's wise idea, and a few months later I was sitting down on my computer writing *Heaven Moves*. The words flew right out of me so quickly, that by three months I thought I was almost done. Little did I know that it would take several years of studying and more of the Lord shaping me to complete this work, and that the dance training program was just the seed to develop a much larger dream called Dancing Waters. I have learned so much since then about dance and about the Kingdom. A book was not in my plans, but God knows what He is doing even when we don't!

What you will read in the following pages flows directly from the professional knowledge gained through my studies at Palm Beach Atlantic University, but also from the intimate place in which God taught me how to humbly remain open to his instruction, and through the years slowly (or abruptly) shifted my vision of what dance in the Kingdom of God should look like. My special time dancing with Jesus transformed into a river into which I could dive deep, and facilitate others into. A river in which there is a relationship with Him as a dance partner; a partner not just in technical dance, but in life; a partner to trust fully.

The first form of dance I was ever exposed to was within the church and it wasn't until later that I learned about dance in the secular sphere. As a child I was taught about a simple dance ministry that was only in its beginnings in the Church. I also learned about ballet for a few years in my childhood but it was not until college that I began to take the craft more seriously. I have since witnessed immense change both in the church and in me spiritually and physically. I have been dancing for almost 18 years in the church now, and I have been swept up in the revelatory wave of prophetic movement that has arisen – and boy, am I surfing! I hope to communicate in most practical terms this revolution Holy Spirit has caused within me for the last few years; an adventure which I also encourage you to embark on.

We are beings that were created to operate on the earth, yet we are simultaneously citizens of Heaven. Sometimes it is difficult to understand how both dimensions could be active in our lives. Through the discipline and the art of dance, I have been able to see more clearly the way that our bodies are supposed to manifest the kingdom of God just as much as the other areas of our lives. This book was written with the intention of addressing the alignment of our entire beings, in both aspects of living, in Heaven and on earth.

As well as addressing holistic alignment and strengthening, I intend to share with you a much deeper vision; one of the movement of the church body. The church is a body, and it is also being aligned. The bride is learning how to dance with her Partner; calling the nations to healing, and celebrating the coming of her Groom.

INTRODUCTION

If you're anything like me and like scribbling in your books and writing notes in the margins, I want to give you a heads up. I included a journal in the back of this book because it is supposed to be a practical workbook and tool just as much as it is a great read. So before anything, I ask you to open up your heart, mind, and spirit. Listen to Jesus as He speaks to you through the words on these pages, and allow Him to renew your mind and body through meditation on His love, life, and word. When He speaks to you or you want to speak to Him, I encourage you to write it down in the back. Of course, you are still very welcome to the margins! I pray that as you read and discover you will create discipline in your secret life with Him, and discipline in your soul and body as well.

Originally I began writing this book with a simple idea which was to teach non-dancers how to train their bodies and their spirits through one book, and not several different pieces of material. As I wrote and explored and really dove into this dream, Jesus expanded it far more than I could have ever imagined. This book has become something weighty and challenging to write; but it is that much more rewarding to have completed it.

This book turned out much more to be about a holistic approach to moving with the Spirit of God. As a dancer, I have realized that many disciplines I apply physically have spiritual applications too, and it was easy to draw parallels between the two in my mind. I simply want to share them with you. When I use the term holistic I just refer to moving with the Lord using all of our being; our whole being—spirit, soul, and body. Aside from this main topic, I felt the Spirit leading me to write about His bride. Yes, the body! There is a greater prophetic parallel hidden within the breaths of this book, and it calls out to the bride of Jesus Christ. Let's move with Him. Let's learn how to listen and love and trust in a fully yielded partnership.

SECTION ONE

DANCE AND HEAVEN

MOVEMENT VS. STAGNATION – THE SWAMP

Humanity must move to survive. Anything that is alive needs to move, no matter how hard it tries not to. Plants' microscopic cells swish around inside their stems. Animals run and hunt and play. Our lungs, our heart beat, our blood rushing through our veins – they are all indicators that we are alive. We breathe. We move. We live.

Without movement, we become stagnant and stinky, like a swamp. Although it may sound simple, this is essential. This points out that it is part of our purpose to move, because it is part of our innate nature. If something alive doesn't move, it stagnates, rots, and eventually dies. The purpose behind movement is to bring life, not to destroy it. I believe that movement has the same spiritual application as it does physically, and in the beginning of the Bible we can see why.

DANCE WAS CREATED IN HEAVEN

To better understand "Why a book about dance?" and "Why now?" I would like to excavate the origin of dance and speak about the time the church has come to now within history. Dance was born in the heart of God. He designed it with a specific purpose, and I firmly believe that it is part of His very essence. In Genesis 1:1-2 it says:

> "In the beginning God created the heavens and the earth. And the earth was waste and void; and darkness was upon the face of the deep: and the Spirit of God *moved* upon the face of the waters."[1]

Before the beginning of man, the Spirit of God created and He *moved*. The Lord is the Creator of the world. He is an artist and His nature is Creator. Then we see that the Holy Spirit Himself was the originator of purposeful movement. He was moving over the face of the waters because He was about to create the universe! Every single time the Holy Spirit moves it is because He is bringing life. So we see, life and motion are intertwined, and the Lord's nature is not stagnant, but fluid. Later on in Genesis we see that we are created in the image of God; meaning that when we *move* we can bring life and create! We have the privilege as sons and daughters of God to co-labor with the greatest Artist and bring life, physically, emotionally, and spiritually through our movement. Although this may be hard for some to believe because of what dance represents in the outside world or in different cultures, it is easier to grasp when we understand that the way the world views dance is a strategy of the enemy who is trying to pervert what God originally made good.

Satan is an imitator, not a creator. He continually takes Heavenly ideas and changes them so that they become twisted, although their nature is originally good. He mixes a little bit of truth with a little bit of lie so we have a hard time telling the difference.[2] His strategy never changes because he isn't creative and therefore doesn't do new things. His goal is to steal, kill, and destroy man.[3] When Adam and Eve decided to disobey God in the garden, they allowed sin to enter the world and it twisted everything which was originally good.[4] Satan has been perverting holy and perfect things through the centuries since. It's pretty easy to recognize this distortion exists just about everywhere. He tries this in and outside of the artistic sphere. Within art, we can see art being distorted and used for existential, nihilistic, and humanistic purposes. Drama, studio art, dance, and music are all used to promote depraved lifestyles focused on self worship, when they were originally created to worship God. Lucifer himself was very possibly an angel of worship[5] before he rebelled and thought that instead of God he should be worshiped[6], which reveals one of the reasons the arts are so attacked by him. The original corruption of art used as worship comes from Satan and the rebellion seed he placed in man. He temped Eve and both man and woman shifted their eyes away from God and onto themselves.[7]

RESTORE THE DESIGN

Whenever art glorifies you and not God, you are growing the seed of pride and presumption that Satan himself had within him when he rebelled before the throne of the Father. This destruction of God's original creative design can be seen in other areas outside art as well. All of this perversion talk might sound discouraging, but on the contrary, it is highlighting a fact: Dance does not come from the world, it comes from God. What I mean is, if we are able to see that Satan is attacking it to twist it all up, it means that it must be originally good. It means He created it. He dreamed of it. And He even participated in it. "Understanding the reality and history of the church and how the enemy has slowly deceived, corrupted, and almost destroyed the gift of spiritual dances, gives us hope for what is possible. And we can be excited in holding onto the knowledge that *GOD DANCES OVER US*, and that its possible to know dance as God originally intended it."[8] Nowadays the world correlates dancing with clubbing, partying, drugs, and sex; but I share with you the Truth— Dance and the arts were dreamed up by the Lord and we as children of God have the responsibility and authority to restore the arts to their original design! Not only is this a calling, but it is an awesome privilege to be able to use arts as they were meant to be used – for worship, light, and love!

The church has never lived a time like it is living now. There is a greater number of Christians on the earth now than ever before. Miracles and revivals are exponentially growing all over the world. We have entered the last days, where wicked people will be weeded out and judged.[9] Darkness is increasing, but so is the light. The church is getting restless in her slumber, and is finally awakening to heal a broken and lost world.[10] We must do what we are called to do and say yes to the Lord, and those who have gifts in the arts and know that God has directed them towards the arts need to know that life, freedom, healing, revival, and so much more will come through them to millions of people hungering for God on the earth. The Spirit of God will pour Himself out through us and to starving nations, rich and poor.

> "For the creation waits with eager longing for the revealing of the sons of God" (Romans 8:19)

HEAVENLY IMPACT

Different personal experiences have led me to understand how dance is actually not from earth but that it was originated in Heaven and can therefore have a heavenly impact on those who view it. Through dance I have been able to see people healed, chains broken, and conviction brought to the hardest of hearts. I've also had my share of fun times dancing with children on the streets or even with angels as the Lord opened my eyes to see them and move with them. This was around the time when Jesus had begun to teach me about seeing angels during worship sessions, listening to them, watching them, copying their movement and collaborating with them to worship our King. I was in a moment of spontaneous worship on Sunday morning when I saw a crowd of angels all around me; moving wherever I went. They were supporting me in dance at that moment. It was like a flock of birds surrounding me. During those few moments, as I jumped off of the ground, I saw them fly up all around me; their effort lifting me up higher than I would usually ever jump, and suspending me for longer than I have ever been in the air. It was such a memorable experience for me! During these years I began to start to tap in to the understanding that Heaven and dance really coexist, and that our bodies could be used as incredible tools for the Kingdom of God. From then to now, I have seen time and time again how dance has opened up the hard hearts to receiving a message of hope and salvation. I have experienced first hand emotional healing through dance, and have also seen a child receive love and hope through dance as well.

DANCE IN THE CHURCH AND BIBLE

The Church in its beginnings widely accepted dance. "Christians were accustomed to celebrating, in dance, at worship and festivals because the Hebrew tradition of dance was so strong."[11] We see that the early church always accepted dancing, as dancing was a typical form of joyful and worshipful expression. Around the 4th century, things began to change. During the time of the expansion of the Roman Empire, especially the rule of Constatine, the Church rejected dance due to the idea that it was of the secular world. The clergy did this with intentions of wanting to purify the church from the pagan customs of the time, which involved crude and licensious dancing. During the early and late middle ages, there were still tight restrictions on dance within the church. Throughout the Renaissance, the Church still sought to quiet dance, although allowing it in calculated circumstances, so it was during the time of the Protestant Reformation that it was completely snuffed out. Dance was then reintroduced into the Protestant belief very slowly after the Great Awakening and there are still many churches and denominations that don't support dance within the church even today.[12]

Although, if we study the word and history, we are able to see that the restrictions and assumptions about dance were only made by man and not by God. In fact, He commanded his people to worship Him through their bodies in the Bible! Fortunately, the Spirit has begun to reveal new things in this prophetic era, and dance is starting to rise with a position of honor in the church. The Church has now begun to recognize this and accept and include dance as worship in the sanctuary once more. Joy comes through dance. Freedom comes through dance. The voice of dance is growing as an art form and as an expression of worship, and Christians worldwide are preparing themselves and practicing prophetic dance; dance for the encouraging and the building up of the body of Christ.[13]

Dance, Biblically, is an expression of joy and celebration to God. Different instances in Biblical history depict different bodily expressions of dancing such as kneeling, jumping, and leaping. Here are a few examples of movement mentioned in the Bible:

"You have turned for me my mourning into **dancing**: you have put off my sackcloth, and girded me with gladness;" (Psalms 30:11)

"Let them praise his name in the **dance**: let them sing praises to him with the tambourine and harp." (Psalms 149:3)

"Rejoice in that day and **leap** for joy, because great is your reward in heaven. For that is how their ancestors treated the prophets. (Luke 6:23)

"Come, let us **bow** down in worship, let us **kneel** before the LORD our Maker;" (Psalm 95:6)

One of my favorite biblical examples is when King David danced for joy in the Lord so hard that all of his royal garments fell off! He stripped himself down of all that represented his status as one of the most powerful kings of the century, and he humbled himself before the Lord; dancing and dancing.

"Wearing a linen ephod, David was **dancing before the LORD with all his might**," (2 Samuel 6:14)

To restore dance and the arts, we must first accept that their origin is heavenly. This unlocks great possibilities in the arts because it means we have the upper hand. We do not have to mimic or copy the artists of the world to "wow the crowds". We get every creative thing straight from the Source. To obtain things from this Source, which is Jesus' Spirit, we must know Him.

IT ALL COMES FROM INTIMACY

It never stops amazing me that the Creator of the entire universe, the eternally present, the author and embodiment of Love, chooses to be vulnerable with His children. *He wants to be known.* True intimacy with the Father implies that you will come before him in complete honesty, transparency, and nakedness as He does with you. It's not a place where you are a doormat, stripped and laid down, and God gets to keep all His fancy clothes on and sit on the throne to use you as a footstool. It is a secret place that He created just for you! This place is a literal secret, because no one else can access it other than you—it is a secret between you and God. No one can go to your secret place except you. This is the place where He lavishes all of His love over you, whispers in your ear, tells you the things you have been longing to hear, and shows you more about yourself.[14] This is the special place where God has and can reveal things to His children who have developed an honest relationship with Him and have security in their identities as sons and daughters. In this place you can mess up, you can fail, you can cry out, laugh, or just sit in the quiet and enjoy each other. In this place you can learn exactly how it is that the Holy Spirit moves in and around you. There is room for error because there is no fear in the manifest love of intimacy.[15]

Through the prayers of saints that have come from these secret birthplaces, dance has evolved and aligned with Heaven so that the spiritual realm and the artist world can align and bring glory to God our Father with a true spirit of worship.[16] I cannot stress enough the importance of this aspect of the normal Christian life. God is so personal, and although He created us for community with other humans, we first and foremost need to know how to relate to Him; accept His love and give Him unrestrained love in return. This will edify you beyond belief, and will make you look and move more and more like Him each day.

I began my technical career as a dancer much later in life than most, but my professors always told me how shocked they were at my rapid growth and my seemingly trained body. In all honesty, if I had not asked the Lord to take control of me and strengthen me every day of my college career as I took all of these new dance classes, I would have never improved as rapidly as I did. My relationship with Him came first, and that even caused an impact on how much I improved and received in class physically—not to mention the hours I spent dancing with Him alone in my room!

"But when you pray, go into your room and shut the door and pray to your Father **who is in secret**. And your Father who sees in secret will reward you." (Matthew 6:6)

"But it was to us that God revealed these things by his Spirit. For his Spirit searches out everything and **shows us God's deep secrets**." (1 Corinthians 2:10)

LISTEN

When we spend time in the secret place with the Holy Spirit, it is important not just to talk to Him about what we want to say; but to listen. After all, He is God and He knows far better than us what He is doing!

"God has been around a long time, and He has had a long time to think about you. He's been living in the experience of knowing you long before you were ever born. He doesn't just have a few random thoughts about you here and there. For trillions of years, God has been thinking about you, and the Holy Spirit searches that whole archive and brings incredible treasures to you at precisely the right moment—if you're listening." [17]

If you were about to cross the road and you heard

something that sounded like an 18 wheeler zooming towards you but you didn't see it, your physical reaction would be to jump back off the road! Even if you couldn't see the truck, but you heard it, you would react and your heart would race.

Often times the Lord wants us to do the same exact thing when He speaks to us. But, hearing physically is usually a lot easier than listening spiritually.

One day I was backing out of a parking space with my music blaring in the car. I looked in my mirrors and reversed, the coast looked clear, but I wasn't being extremely cautious. Once I was almost fully out on the road I felt a "thump". It couldn't be! I hit a truck that was backing up at the same time as me that was in a blind spot. It was one of those trucks with the loud and obnoxious "Beep! Beep! Beep!" as it reverses, but I didn't hear it! My music was too loud. If only I had my windows cracked open, I would have heard it. I thought back and remembered hearing a faint beeping before the crash, but I didn't really listen to it above all of the other noise around me.

When we listen to the Lord, we have to make sure that we tone down all of the noise around us. We need to give him space to speak to us; even if that means cracking your window just a bit so the sound of His warnings can slip in. To hear Him, we must shift our focus from our own loud emotions, thoughts, and even our culture to what He is saying outside of our own car.

Listen to Him, because He has amazing things to tell you. Now there is also a way to listen not just with your spirit, but with your body.

ALIGNMENT

Humans are three part beings. They are composed of a spirit (essence of life and connection point with God), which has a soul (mind, will, emotions) that lives in a body (physical flesh bound to space and time). As Christians, we are often taught at church to live in the Spirit and not satisfy the desires of our flesh.[18] We also learn not to allow our emotions dominate our choices but to choose the Lord's truth over our own. But as dancers, we must learn to yield our *bodies* to our spirits so that what is coming from the Holy Spirit can be channeled through our physical bodies, not just our spirits and souls.

1 Corinthians 2 talks about the Spirit of God and how only the Spirit of God can know the deep things of God. We learn through the same passage that through Jesus Christ we have access in our spirits to God's very Spirit, meaning we can also know the deep things of God and have the mind of Christ. This is extremely important, because dance training in the Kingdom involves *aligning our spirits first* to be in unity with the Spirit of God so that our movement can flow from Him. So, our body yields to our soul, which must yield to our spirits, which are in accord with the Spirit of God.

Here are two examples of improper alignment:

The first would look something like dancing out of your emotions in the moment. It could look very nice, but it isn't the Holy Spirit that's moving you. Please don't misunderstand me, emotions are part of us and part of expressing yourself as a dancer, but if you want to dance as a Kingdom vessel, then emotions are not what should move you. The Spirit's movement should lead you, to which then your emotions respond or are a part of, and your body reflects it. Spirit. Soul. Body. In that order. This means that your emotions are fully involved and engaged, but they are not taking control of the situation. This goes to say for the mind as well. It should be engaged, but not in control of your being; Jesus should have that seat.

The second example would be a common comfort zone that many trained dancers may have. This is letting their bodies lead their movement. These dancers are used to certain movements and have a developed muscle memory or movement vocabulary, so they can move led by that instead of by the Spirit. Again, although it isn't necessarily wrong to dance this way, it isn't the true goal either.

I am giving examples that are really specific to dancing right now, but holistic alignment doesn't just apply to dancers. It applies to everyone. I think it's a lot easier to experience this alignment when you dance because you are aware of your body at all times when moving, so its easier to pinpoint how that third part of our being needs to be aligned. I thought I could also share with you a few examples of the body being in misalignment outside of the realm of dance, to show you the importance of keeping our bodies in check with the Spirit in daily life, too.

And now, for a comical short story by Stephanie Barrera:

Sally enters her kitchen after an exhausting day of work. Not only did she take her kids to soccer after school and then out for ice cream, which she valiantly resisted eating, but she then slipped on her Nikes and went to the gym, diligently following her New Year's resolution.

Back at home with her stomach gurgling, she opens up the fridge searching for her smoothie mix, and puts it in the magic bullet with some ice and.... kale. She gulps it down, wincing, but it's not enough to satisfy the rumbling in her tummy. "Now what?" she thinks.

And then, what's this?! She sees the box: The beautiful hot pink, orange, and white box with the heavenly Dunkin Donuts logo on top. Her hand, moving on its own, swings the box open! Her nose smiles at the delectable aroma. A fresh dozen. With sprinkles.

Before she knows it, two donuts have been inhaled and her New Year's resolution reset to start—tomorrow.

We have all been there! Our bodies can often rule what we do, especially when we are tired and hungry. Sally here is a perfect example of not listening to the Spirit and letting her body dictate her choice. In our daily life choices, as well as in dance, we must stop and listen to the Spirit and submit to what He tells us. It's a beautiful and spontaneous form of fasting, even. I confess, often times I feel the Spirit telling me to actually *eat* the donut! I am usually way too hard on myself, and I think many dancers can relate, and I deprive myself of all sugary, sprinkled, pleasures. Yet the Lord loves when we enjoy life too, and sometimes eating the donut is my form of alignment to Him. Hunger is not the only desire that our bodies produce, and our fleshly desires can be vicious! It takes discipline that sprouts from true love of the Lord to kill the desires of the flesh and submit them to Him.[19]

If we are able to align the three parts of our being so that our spirits are in charge, our souls are submitted to our spirits, and our bodies are reflecting that, we will receive and execute what Jesus is trying to communicate. Even through a rehearsed piece that includes muscle memory, the Spirit can still reign if that is how you align your being. When we allow Him to move us that is when deliverance through the body comes. That is when Kingdom movement establishes light in places of darkness. That is when God receives the utmost glory. That is when new movement is revealed to us. We can learn about physical alignment all we want, and we can train the body all we would like, but if we do not allow our bodies and souls to focus on the Spirit of God, we will never reach our maximum potential as vessels of the living God.

> **Journal Prompt:** Play some worship music in your own room, and focus on yielding your body to the Spirit. See what happens to your movement and write it down. If it's hard for you to yield your body to His movement, that's okay too. Write down your results!

Alignment and listening when you dance is not only important for developing a new movement vocabulary, but also for being able to discern the movement of the Spirit during a church service, when choreographing, or when choosing a venue. Different movements, when executed correctly and on time with the movement of the Spirit can cause shakings in the spiritual realm and in the lives of those spectating. When we are obedient to the Holy Spirit as we are dancing, our very bodies become physical manifestations of the Kingdom. Think about that! Our literal bodies can wholly be used as vessels carrying and piercing this world with a bit of Heaven. We have been given that privilege as sons and daughters. Talk about Heaven touching earth!

"May God himself, the God of peace, sanctify you through and through. May your whole spirit, soul and body be kept blameless at the coming of our Lord Jesus Christ." (1 Thess. 5:23)

YOUR BODY IS THE TEMPLE

Something that continually blows my mind is that my physical body can be an actual manifestation of the Kingdom of Heaven while I am on the earth. If we are aligned as I have talked about in the above sections, our bodies as part of our being, although naturally sinful and bound to the laws of earth, can transform into glory carrying vessels that actually pierce the earth's atmosphere with the atmosphere of the Kingdom. What?! God amazes me with His awesome grace that He would even allow us, what's more, desire for us, to share in His Kingdom and being a part of establishing it on earth. When you dance and you are aligned to His spirit, you don't only "make people cry" or "look nice". You bring Heaven down. You become a portal from another dimension in which Light has full authority and reign.

The word says that we are the temples of the Holy Spirit. Understanding that we literally house the Sprit and physically represent the Kingdom also increases the awareness that we should have about what we allow our bodies to do and not to do. Sins that involve the body, like sexual sin, fornication, pornography, gluttony, eating disorders, self-harm, and other bodily sins cause a tremendous hindrance in how much we can receive from the Lord and how well we can align our bodies to the spiritual realm. When we do positive things to and with the body, such as exercising, sleeping well, fueling our bodies correctly, and even fasting, it has the opposite effect; giving us a keen awareness of what the Lord wants to do, and allowing for a more easily yielded body to the Spirit, because it knows discipline. It is absolutely incredible that God chose us and our physical bodies to dwell in. Our bodies are actually the temples of the Holy Spirit, and as carriers of His glory, we need to take care of that temple.

"[This] I say then, Walk in the Spirit, and ye shall not fulfill the lust of the flesh." (Galatians 5:16-17)

"Don't you realize that your body is the temple of the Holy Spirit, who lives in you and was given to you by God? You do not belong to yourself," (1 Corinthians 6:19)

"Therefore, I urge you, brothers and sisters, in view of God's mercy, to offer your bodies as a living sacrifice, holy and pleasing to God—this is your true and proper worship." (Romans 12:1)

WORSHIP AND DANCE

I've mentioned worship a lot up until now, but I haven't really dived into what I exactly mean when I say worship. This is how I teach my kiddos about worship. I use my pointer finger: Worship is when **God** (pointing up) is number **one** (holding finger out in #1 sign) in **our** (pointing to all) **hearts**! (pointing to my chest). Although this is something that seems simple and silly, it is a profound truth that has managed to confront me hundreds of times in my life. If we'd only let the One we love sit on the throne 24/7! I can't even imagine what the Church would accomplish!! We must live worshiping in spirit and truth, always. Worship is a lifestyle that demonstrates that God's opinion matters more than your own and that He truly has control over every part of your life. Sometimes worship can be mistaken for a session of music in a church service, but actually, it is a position of the heart; that position is laid down flat (surrender!). One's actions will always reflect the position of the heart and manifest themselves in an outer expression of worship. If your actions do not exactly match up with honoring the Lord, the probability is that you are worshipping yourself! Some examples of a laid down heart of worship are unwavering obedience, alone time spent with God, sowing and giving, prayer, service, fellowship, and music. Dance, as you may have guessed it, is also one of these manifestations of worship! And one of my favorites!

Your worship of God only goes as far as your revelation of God. This is something I was taught by my dad from a young age, and I have come to understand it as my relationship with the Lord has deepened over the years and trials of my life. It's simple. If God has only revealed Himself as my Savior to me, then I will worship Him as a Savior. I will be limited to worshipping Him as a Savior until I come to *know* Him as more than that. It can take a sick family member coming to health or my hurting heart to be healed for me to worship him as Healer, because I come to know Him in that way. If one day it is revealed to me by His word that I am no longer called His servant, but His friend, then I will worship Him as a friend, too. My worship of Him grows as my understanding of Him grows. This entire concept shows us that knowing God and worshipping God are inseparably linked.

THE PRESUMPTUOUS ARTIST

Now of course, not all dancing is worship, just as not all the times we sing and clap our hands is worship. If the attitude of your heart is incorrect, dancing can be idolatrous just as much as it can be worship. It is very easy to start placing your identity in what you do as a dancer, instead of in Christ. Your heart can become addicted to seeking glory for yourself, and pride can attack you from behind without you even realizing it if you aren't careful to wear humility. You will have a hard fall if you begin to believe that what you have is because you are so gifted. Talents are gifts of God, and given by pure grace. These gifts were only given to us to share with others in love. Here I specifically want to warn dancers reading who have taken part in dance ministries and companies before: Pride about being up on a stage can bite you hard. Always keep a humble heart, and take care to see that your worship is the same on the stage as well as off it. The moment you dance on stage but are not cultivating that intimate relationship with Jesus, get off for your own good! Dance can only be true worship if it is centered on the One whom we are worshiping. In this current age, dance can also be perverted and can even open doors to sin and darkness. Dance was originally created as an expression of worship and the children of God are being called to promote the Kingdom, not to promote themselves.

Whether one takes part in a dance ministry or not, it is still important to know that just as He moves, we should also move; and that genuine worship can be expressed through movement of the body, and is even commanded by God.

Our worship should be true and never feigned for others to see and compliment us on. God seeks those who worship

Him in spirit and truth. [16]

There are several forms to show one's worship through dance. Within the church, this is most commonly done as special performances with the purpose of ministry, or a dance team that dances during the musical section of the service. I by no means intend to say that this is the only outlet dance that should be used as worship. In fact, one of my favorite ways to worship the Lord through dance is outside of the church building. We are commissioned to go and be the light in the world which can also be done through being part of a secular company or a dance group with a Kingdom focus. Using dance to spread the gospel or cause awareness for social justice issues, for example, is an amazing and admirable form of worship too. Let's not forget that dance is not just meant to be kept within the body of Christ, but that it is one of the greatest tools of proclaiming Truth to the people in the world through a cross-cultural art form.

BREAKING THE BOX

My curiosity, questioning, independence and stubbornness can many times be a downside of mine, but when it comes to breaking religious structures, these character qualities come mighty in handy. I love this section. I was born for this. I wasn't born to follow the norm or to do what everybody else does. The Church is not called to do what everyone else does or to stay the same year after year, either. It is called to lead the world to Light and Love, with creativity and freedom far beyond anyone in the world can fathom. This section was specifically written for all of my fellow ministry dancers. As I said, I am a very curious person in nature, and I like to understand the "why" of my faith. Over the past five years in my own secret places of prayer, I have asked questions about our church dance department. If you've asked yourself or God these questions, don't be alarmed! It isn't a bad thing. Questions like: Why is it that we...

- wear *these* dance costumes/ garments?
- do *these* moves?
- dance *on* stage?
- dance at *all*?
- use dance *instruments*?
- use *choreography*?
- use *spontaneous/ improvised* dance?
- do the *same thing* for years?

These among many, many, more. As I searched for answers from the Lord and did my own research, I came to realize that many of the traditions we hold in liturgical dance ministry came from a heart of worship but were only meant for a season, and the Lord is now working in a new season. When it comes to movement and art, I always try to keep the verse in Isaiah in mind when the Lord says, "Behold, I am doing a new thing; now it springs forth, do you not perceive it?"[20] The last thing I would want is for God to be doing something better than the season before and to miss it! My prayer for myself and for the Church is that we do not miss out on the new thing God is doing with the uncovering of dance in the church and in the marketplace. We sometimes have to break our old box—the way we think things should be—so that we can accept the new things God is doing. The old is almost always never compatible with the new. The verse preceding the one I just quoted, says: "Remember not the former things, nor consider the things of old". Through this I understood that some of the dance structures we uphold are inherited patterns that may inhibit a new move of God in your worship. If you haven't asked similar questions to these mentioned above, I encourage you to do so! If you have, do not feel bad or alone. I plead that you would open up your mind, because it is about time that we stop limiting the Holy Spirit and how He can use us in the artistic realm within the Church. There is so much He wants to do with us, and all we have to do is heed to his supernatural movement! He will blow us out of the water, and He will shine through us to a crooked and depraved world.

As a disclaimer, I by no means try to claim that God is not the same today as He was yesterday. I believe the Lord is always the same, yet He is definitely a God that *moves*. The Lord moves constantly and we must learn to jump into that river, submerge completely, and flow with Him. Sometimes that may be different or scary, but it is always good! I invite you not just to dip your toes in the water, not just to go knee deep, but to give up control fully and allow the Lord's waters of life to rush over your head.

Breaking our box pushes us into dependency on God. I think that is a major reason why He continually changes things in our lives. He does it so that we don't get too comfortable and start relying on our own strength. Bill Johnson puts it so well in his book, The Supernatural Power of a Transformed Mind when he says, "You'll know when He is speaking... It will always be better than anything you could have thought up yourself. And if He gives you new ideas, they will probably be impossible for you to accomplish in your own strength. His thoughts will so overwhelm you that you'll want to draw close to Him so they can be accomplished."[21]

"Neither is new wine put into old wineskins. If it is, the skins burst and the wine is spilled and the skins are destroyed. But new wine is put into fresh wineskins, and so both are preserved." (Matthew 9:17)

"Therefore, if anyone is in Christ, the new creation has come: The old has gone, the new is here!" (2 Corinthians 5:17)

"...and then led me through the water, and it was ankle-deep. 4 Again he measured a thousand, and led me through the water, and it was knee-deep. Again he measured a thousand, and led me through the water, and it was waist-deep. 5 Again he measured a thousand, and it was a river that I could not pass through, for the water had risen. It was deep enough to swim in, a river that could not be passed through." (Ezekiel 47:3-5)

PROPHETIC DANCE — A HEAVENLY TONGUE

"Obedience is a signal to God that says, 'God, I want to go the next step.' That tender heart draws the spirit of revelation to a person and/ or to a body of people; they begin seeing and hearing things they never heard or saw before." [22]

(*Supernatural Power of a Transformed Mind*)

Dance is a communicative form that is perceived through

sight. Different motions compose movement vocabulary, which express different things according to those motions. Throughout the years, people have created, written down, and perfected what I like to call dance "languages" (or genres) such as Ballet, Tap, Jazz, Ballroom, Hip Hop and Modern Dance. Through these languages different dancers have learned to speak and communicate different things to the world around them. If you think about it, this actually comes very inherently to the human being. Think of a young toddler bouncing up and down or moving their little bootie because he or she is so excited that they just got a new toy. This is most commonly known as the "happy dance". The dancing communicates that the baby is happy!

Most usually dancers, or even non-dancers, are accustomed to a specific movement vocabulary (hopefully more than just bouncing up and down and moving your bootie around). As the Lord continues to bring fresh things to His people, the Spirit of God causes a desire in the hearts and spirits of dancers for a different movement vocabulary. I like to compare this occurrence to the gift of tongues. Go with me on this. Humans are usually accustomed to speaking and thinking in their own language; in this case, English. When the Holy Spirit comes upon a person and gives him or her the gift of Heavenly tongues, the person receiving it cannot be afraid of error or not understanding what is happening. They just have to *let go*. Likewise, there is a moment in a dancer's life where they can decide to let Holy Spirit teach them a new Heavenly language, but they cannot be afraid of error or of the unknown. You just have to let go! When Holy Spirit began to teach me this personally, I spent 20 minutes allowing him to slowly "move" my arm during an organic worship session that broke out during a rehearsal. I experimented as I stood and opened my spiritual ears, and all of my nerve endings, so that I could be moved into a dance vocabulary that I was not used to.

Eventually this way of experimenting with the Lord evolved to just allowing Him to move my whole body with full confidence. It led to amazing times of new movement discoveries as I was literally amazed at what I was executing, without ever having done anything like it. I am sure that I would have never thought to have done movements such as these, and if I had, they would definitely not have been so cleanly and swiftly performed. It is truly an exhilarating and other-worldly experience.

My experience, I believe, can pave the way for many others. I do not think that you have to wait for twenty minutes just moving your arm, because you have this book that the Lord can use to guide you and expedite the process. Remember that no one taught me this stuff but the Lord Himself.

Moving with Him like this doesn't just happen for the sole purpose of spontaneous dancing, but the Lord can teach new movement for choreography as well. I used to choreograph for our dance department, and one of my favorite things to do was to watch the girls on the team dance as they were led by the Spirit, and start using the movements the Lord gave them and incorporate them into choreography and our prophetic movement vocab.

I also obviously believe technique is very important. Technique is used as a way to polish movement, cleanly execute it, and to prevent injury. It is an amazing tool that takes our dance to new levels of excellence and artistry, and if you feel called to the professional world, you need to know technique and practice it with great care.

A word about experimenting with new dance movements: If it is your first time "listening" to the Spirit with your body, experimentation is best done in a safe environment like a rehearsal or your personal time with the Lord. This way you don't have to be worried about what the surrounding audience may or may not think, keeping the integrity of the worship pure. Make sure that there are no pointy objects around (be safe!) and try to embrace a spirit of adventure (have fun)! Be like a child and curiously ask the Holy Spirit for new, interesting, movements!

"All of them were filled with the Holy Spirit and began to speak in other tongues as the Spirit enabled them." (Acts 2:4)

DANCE IN THE MARKETPLACE

Have you ever been in a dark room when suddenly someone turns on their phone screen? It is very difficult to ignore a light in a dark place. I've proven this true in many different occasions; light is just something that attracts humans. When there is a fire, people watch it. When it is dark and someone shines a flashlight, people gravitate towards it. Even when someone turns on their cellphone in a movie theater, people turn their heads.

I have come to understand that dance is like a light in a dark place. It is extremely hard to ignore a dancer. Picture you and your friend or family walking down the sidewalk. All of a sudden on the other side of the road, there is a person dancing around. It is hard not to stare! Dance is hard to ignore because dance is like a light. Dance is a communicative form, therefore the people walking down the street and watching that dancer have then received a message from that person, whether they like it or not. This message could have been positive or negative, but it was sent and it was also received through sight. Dance doesn't need music, and it doesn't need a language. It impacts more deeply than just the mind, and it reaches the soul and even the spirit. It could be that people watch you dance and don't understand what they are seeing, but they feel something. That is the power of dance.

I have often seen many dance ministries form within the Church and preach that it is wrong to "perform" because it takes the glory away from God, but I see it a bit differently. Firstly, this is based on what your definition of the word *performance* is. Performing defined as putting on a show that causes you to be glorified is not rooted in a heart of worship. But, there is another way to perform for the glory of God. I see performance as shining your light. There are dancers out there who are commissioned specifically to perform in parks, theatres, and non-Christian settings so that they can bring messages of hope and truth to their audiences. After all, what is a better place to shine a light than in the dark?

My personal dream is to use dance to speak for those who do not have voices because of their physical or emotional conditions. People enslaved or persecuted around the world need to tell their stories, and I have been given a body and a gift to be able to communicate that to the world *and* to the Church, so as to bring justice to perishing nations. Dance brings healing and dance brings people to Jesus. There are many people out there who can come to a performance and encounter the Holy Spirit just because the dancers yielded their bodies and lives for that very purpose.

"...that you may be blameless and innocent, children of God without blemish in the midst of a crooked and twisted generation, among whom you **shine as lights in the world**" (Philippians 2:15)

It is important to understand that a dancer can be called within the Church, but also outside of it. It is very possible that one dancer can be called to overt ministry through dance, and another to covert ministry in Hollywood. This doesn't mean that the dancer is hiding their faith, it just means that their vocation is in the "secular" world, but it is still for the upbuilding of the Kingdom. This should actually be true for all Christians and not just dancers; our careers should be surrendered to the Lord for the purpose of edifying the Kingdom and reaching the nations for Jesus Christ. This position and the uncovering of God-glorifying dance in the Church and in the marketplace has risen up, because of people who have not been afraid to push the limits and have searched for the heart of God and the movement of Heaven in their own secret places. If you've read all of this so far and have asked yourself, "but how can I do this?" don't forget the answer is: It all comes from *intimacy*.

DANCE AND INTERCESSION

Especially as dancers shining light in the dark places, intercessory prayer is a must. The Bible says that our battle is not against flesh and blood, but against the principalities and powers in the heavenly realms.[23] Praying continually as you move opens up the Heavens and increases the ability to hear the Lord. Sometimes God will lay a specific thing to intercede for on the heart of the dancer, and give them a supernatural way of interpreting that prayer burden with their bodies. Sometimes these burdens can be for individuals and sometimes it can be directed for the congregation. As dancers that represent the Kingdom of Light, we must continually have in mind that if the Lord reveals something dark about an individual whom we are interceding for through movement, we do not want to encourage the spirit of darkness. For example, if the person is bound by a spirit of depression, the dance should not be sad and discouraging. Rather, the movement should be breaking the depression, uplifting, and hopeful. We should never dance darkness over others; we always move to encourage the body of Christ, not to confuse it. This goes specifically when dancing over others during times of ministry.

I am not saying that dance should always be happy and not depict hardship. If this were true, we would never be able to tell the stories of the many men and women trapped in sex slavery, for example, but when dancing over people during a worship or healing service, it is important to remember that we are there to uplift our brothers and sisters.

The Lord might even lead you to intercede through dance for a different nation. At about age twenty God began to give me different tongues of different nations as I interceded for them. One day, I felt I should move my body as I prayed for Asia, and I danced something that looked to me like a native Indian dance. My hands, fingers, and even my eyes moved so specifically that I was blown out of the water. I had never been taught those movements or ever in my life had executed them, but I am so sure that the Spirit led me to move like those young girls in India that usually dance for their gods.

WINDOWS OF OPPORTUNITY

Throughout the years I've had several experiences I have come to call *Windows of Opportunity*. A Window of

Opportunity is when God shows a person an opportunity to do something He would like for them to do before it actually happens or in the moments right before it happens. The person can either choose to do what God has shown them, causing a breakthrough or shifting point, or continue on his own comfortable path. Windows of Opportunity show up everywhere in life, but in the dance realm they look something like this: Picture an action movie. The main character is running towards train tracks and the train is coming. He only has a small opening and if he second guesses himself, he will miss his chance to get to the other side. If he doesn't jump quickly enough, he might miss the chance. A similar thing happens to us dancers. During a worship set, a dancer might be leading their team and feel like the Lord is telling them to do something new. This can look like a picture in their mind or just a feeling, and it can come to mind minutes before, or that very second. The leader then has to make a choice: Maybe the team won't understand because it's new. Maybe it has to do with a new movement that the leader has not done before. Maybe it incorporates the crowd. Sooner or later, the window will pass and the moment will have gone. When the Lord presents a window of opportunity, we have to JUMP through. Otherwise, we miss the chance of something new or fresh the Lord is trying to do for the people or for us in a service. For this to happen successfully, we must always keep our spiritual ears open to the Holy Spirit. Do not be afraid. Also, don't be hard on yourself if you miss one. I think I have probably learned just as much or even more from missed windows than I have from the ones I jumped through. God's grace is good!

When specifically in a church service, we also have to be sensitive to the timing and flow of the service. God may show you something before it will happen, and you may have to wait for the actual window to come up. You don't want to jump before the window is there, because you'll just smash headfirst into a brick wall.

Also, submitting to the leader always trumps experimenting with the Spirit in service. There have been occasions where I have felt my leader doing something that I felt wasn't what God wanted at the time. It doesn't matter. Through obedience and submission, the window may have "passed" but the window for your growth in character and authority was jumped through.

> "My dear brothers and sisters, take note of this: **Everyone should be quick to listen**, slow to speak and slow to become angry." (James 1:19)

STILLNESS

I have come across many dance ministries that seem to always move all the time. That sounds funny, because it is expected for a dance team to move, but this is actually not what we should always do. Even as a professional dancer, sometimes we forget that moments of stillness can be beautiful and allow the viewers to process what they have just seen. Choreographically, it is breathtaking and important to have moments of stillness. Going into a deeper spiritual reality than that, sometimes the Holy Spirit requires stillness. When it is hard to hear, it is sometimes better to stop moving than to think dancing will impress anyone or clarify the situation. Sometimes all the Lord wants to do is to shine, and all we have to do is be still and get out of the way. Do not be afraid of stillness, because I have seen some of the most powerful moments in a service happen through the sensitivity of the worship team to stillness and quiet. I have also had some of the most impacting and tender words from Jesus when I have quieted and stilled my soul.

"He says, '**Be still**, and know that I am God; I will be exalted among the nations, I will be exalted in the earth.'" (Psalms 46:10)

ENDNOTES

1. ASV, emphasis added
2. See Genesis 3:1-4 and Matthew 4:1-11
3. John 10:10
4. Genesis 1-3
5. Ezekiel 28:13
6. Isaiah 14:12-15
7. Genesis 3:6, 22
8. "The History of Dance in the Church" – www.refinedundignified.com
9. Matthew 13:40
10. Ephesians 5:14
11. "The History of Dance in the Church" – www.refinedundignified.com
12. "The History of Dance in the Church" – www.refinedundignified.com
13. 1 Corinthians 14:3
14. 1 John 3:1
15. 1 John 4:18
16. John 4:24
17. *The supernatural power of a transformed mind*, Bill Johnson, p.68
18. Romans 13:14
19. Galatians 5:16
20. Isaiah 43:19
21. *The supernatural power of a transformed mind*, Bill Johnson, p.69
22. *The supernatural power of a transformed mind*, Bill Johnson, p.70

BARRERA

SECTION TWO

DANCE ON EARTH

*O God, you are my God, earnestly I seek you; my soul thirsts for you, **my body longs for you**, in a dry and weary land where there is no water.*
Psalm 63:1

Heaven is a realm, just as the physical earth is a realm. In the heavenly realm there are laws, just as there are earthly laws (gravity, physics, etc) on earth. As believers we understand that the law of Heaven is the higher law of the two. Although both the natural and the supernatural operate in our lives, one has a heirachy over the other. God has given us the ability to access Heaven through our spirits, which are housed in our physical bodies. Therefore, we can be used as portals for the Kingdom of Heaven to come to the earth. To more accurately do that, we need to take care of our bodies. This entire section explains why and how we should do that.

Many disciplines that dancers practice can be applied to our spiritual lives. I have found in my journey as a dancer that the lifestyle of a dancer greatly parallels the way the Lord tells us we should live. In this section of the book, you will find sub-sections labeled *"DRAW A PARALLEL"* that highlight how Jesus constantly uses dance to teach me about the Heavenly realm—drawing a parallel between the physical and the supernatural.

You will also find in this section some technical practices which are all based on Modern dance technique, alignment, and execution. Modern dance is an American dance genre that was originally derived from Ballet in the early twentieth century, and since has developed into many branches. From my experience, Modern dance is the easiest introduction to dance for a person who has never danced before. The foundational structures of Modern dance can be applied to any pedestrian movement, so it is helpful even for non-dancers to learn! I hope you enjoy trying some of these practices, and perhaps learn a thing or two about your own body, as well.

ALIGNMENT AND ENGAGEMENT   1

> "May the God of peace himself make you holy in every way. And may your whole being—spirit, soul, and body—remain blameless when our Lord Jesus, the Messiah, appears."
>
> — 1 Thessalonians 5:23

The one part of our three-part beings that is bound to the earth, time, and the laws of earth and time, is the body. So far, we have gone over the alignment of our spiritus, souls and bodies to the Lord. When it comes to dance *on earth*, there is another type of alignment worth addressing: physical alignment. To be a successful dancer, it is important to align the body. Many people think that in order to become a great dancer, they must learn certain dance moves, steps or tricks. However, dance steps are just one of the many things a dancer must learn. Before learning any of those "cool tricks", a dancer must learn to properly align his or her body. There are several reasons why alignment is crucial to the foundation of a dancer: First, alignment prevents injury and allows for an easier flow of breath, and therefore of movement. Second, when a dancer has correct alignment, the muscles develop as they should for a dancer; lean and strong, not short and bulky. Incorrect alignment leads to improper placement, a less pleasing aesthetic, injuries, and a lack of improvement or the stunting of improvement. Essetially, alignment makes movement look good! If you learn and execute proper posture on a daily basis, your body develops strength in a healthy way, and you look good doing it! It isn't always as easy as it seems to stand upright and in proper alignment, but it pays off.

When a dancer is standing upright, correct body alignment looks like this:

Picture a side view of the human body with a vertical line running from top to bottom. The tip of the ear should be in line with the center of the shoulder girdle. The shoulder should be stacked right over the hip, which should be right on top of the back of the knee cap. Lastly, the knee cap should be in line with the center of the heel.

From an aerial view, a line would be drawn straight down the center of the body. The center of the head would be right on top of the center of the spine, which would be over the center of your pelvis, and right between both feet (empty space). It sounds so simple, but amany people actually develop habits throughout their life that are not conducive to proper alignment/posture. As a dancers especially, we need to be aware of our alignment every single day. This allows us to develop healthy habits that translate over to our dance training.

IMPROPER ALIGNMENT

A few common examples of incorrect alignment are demonstrated in the picture below. Many negative effects come from incorrect alignment. The first and most obvious consequence is bad posture leading to aching bones and muscles. In dance, the first problem you will run into when you don't align your body is an injury. Without correct posture, the chances of getting hurt while dancing are much greater. Other such consequences include not being able to improve in technical areas, limited flexibility, limited strength, and an inability to execute steps with a proper quality or aesthetic.

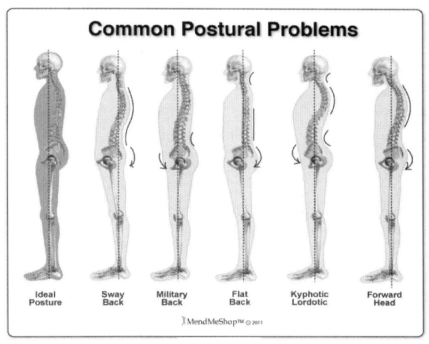

Endnote 2

KNEES OVER YOUR TOES

A very common phrase you will hear dance teachers say is "knees over your toes!" That is a very important alignment tip! Whenever you bend a leg while standing on the floor, you should be able to draw a vertical line from your knee to your toe on that leg that is standing. If your knees are not in line with your toes when your knee is bent, it puts too much tork on your knees and can eventually end up as a major injury!

OFFER UP YOUR HEART

Here is another alignment tip: Press your shoulders down while allowing the muscles in your back to rotate your scapula downwards. Let your head feel lifted so that your neck is stretched. Allow your sternum (the bone in the middle of your chest) to open and lift up, instead of closing in on itself. This helps develop a stronger neck and it prevents improper posture with your head forward, which can cause problems in the spinal discs.

> **Journal Prompt:** Ask a friend to observe your posture when standing or dancing. Taking a picture works too. If you find misalignment, take special consideration of those areas of your body as you go about your day and week. Write about it and how it might change your movement! Practice the excercises on alignment and strengthening and then take another picture in a month or so and see if you can tell the difference.

DRAW A PARALLEL:

Just as we have to have our physical bodies in proper alignment, we need to have our whole beings aligned to the Lord! Dancers can understand alignment in a profound way, because we always have to focus on our physical alignment – and that should remind us of the alignment of our entire being as well – Spirit, soul and body.

Alignment in the physical parallels the natural; and improper alignment does as well. The effects of improper physical alignment include greater risk of injury, not being able to improve in technical areas, limited flexibility, limited strength, and an inability to execute steps with a proper quality or aesthetic. The effects are the same in spiritual alignment. When you are not aligned to the Lord, you have a greater risk of hurting others and causing pain in your own life. Your spiritual growth is stunted by improper alignment, and you also develop bad habits that are increasingly harder to break. Your character is weakened, and even your aesthetic/ quality of life can be lessened if you aren't aligned.

My favorite alignment parallel: I liken the opening of the sternum (chestbone) to offering up my heart to the Lord, and choosing to be vulnerable with Him by exposing my heart.

FRIENDLY MR. SKELETON

To better understand proper alignment, one must know the body. Bones and muscles are especially important to dancers. The function of the Skeletal System is to protect organs and to support the body. Without bones, we would not be able to stand upright. The Muscular System's main function is movement. Muscles are connected to each other and to bones by tendons and ligaments. Dancers should have at least a basic understanding of how muscles and bones move, and where they are in the body. Once you understand where the muscles and bones are, and how they move together, it is easier to understand movement (and to teach it, too).

Look at and study the next few pages. Diagrams of the skeleton and muscles are labeled.

> **Journal Prompt:** Locate the bones and muscles in your own body and move them as individually as you can (this is called isolation). Can you learn something new? Does it feel different to focus on each body part, instead of just moving without that awareness? Which different muscles and bones move together and which ones can you isolate?

Heaven Moves — Alignment and Engagement

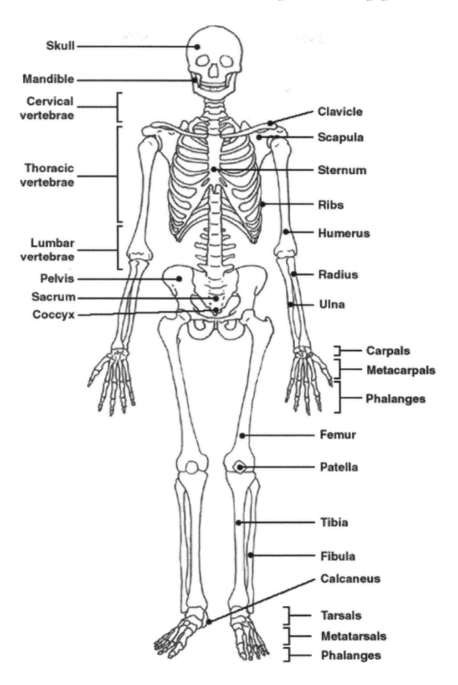

Endnote 3

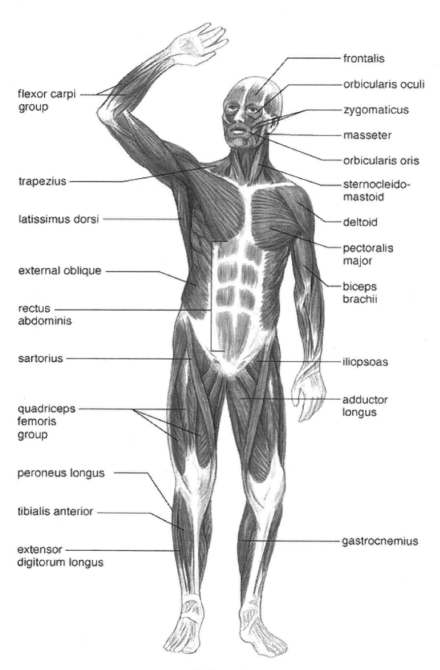

Endnote 4

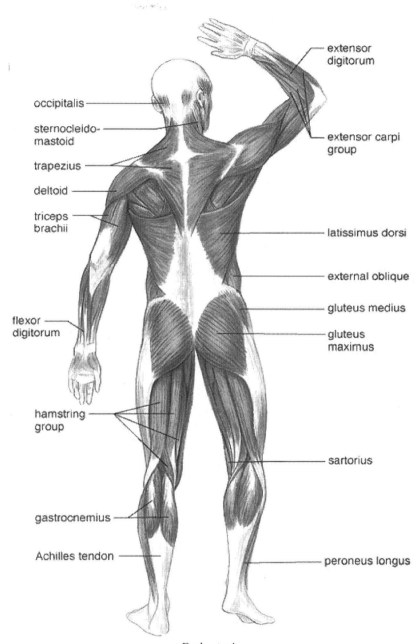

Endnote 4

IT'S ALL ABOUT THAT PELVIS

If you look at the image of the skeleton above, you will notice that the pelvis is the anatomical center of the human body. It is one of the most important body parts in movement because all locomotion involves the pelvis moving from one place to another. Correct alignment of the pelvis means that the dancer will not be tilting it either forward or back. The sitz bones (Those two bones felt when you sit on something hard) should be facing directly towards the floor. When the pelvis is tipped too far forward, it causes a sway back. When it is tipped too far backward, it appears to be "tucked under". It is noticeable that many people have different alignment of the pelvis, but for a dancer, the sitz bones must be facing the floor and there should be no extra curve in the lumbar spine. A good way to help correct improper alignment of the pelvis or lumbar spine is to strengthen the abdominal muscles to keep the spine in its proper place.

Here is American Ballet Theatre's Prima Ballerina's take on alignment and posture:
"Posture, you see, is really all about energy. That is something that we dancers quickly come to understand. We cannot dance fully and freely if our bodies aren't held in a way that allows our breath and energy to circulate, unimpended, from head to toe. That is what gives us our power and ignites the invisible spark that connects ourselves, our fellow dancers, and the audience and that can

help our performances trascend technical precision and soar to a place that is ethereal and magical."[1]

ENERGY FLOW

What exactly is energy? Our bodies are never still. Even though we may stop moving, our cells and atoms are always in constant motion. Much like this, one must always be "in motion" while dancing. This does not mean that one must always be executing dance movements, but that the energy level of a dancer should always remain turned "on" instead of "off". Evidence of life should be shown throughout the body whether it is moving quickly, slowly, or barely at all. Energy isn't just for visual effect. The use of energy helps us to fully embody movement. It helps with balance. It helps with understanding different techniques through the body. The inner workings/muscles of the body release energy; and our expression of movement changes based on the way we release energy. Energy can help develop your artistry as a dancer, too. It is a skill that transcends strength and flexibility and demonstrates maturity in a dancer.

In the diagram below, I depicted what I think of every time I talk about energy. The energy is represented by the arrows, but in my mind looks more like streams of light. When we dance, we should always think of this image, and not only think of it, but embody it. The audience should be able to see the energy flow of the dancer through every single part of the body whether or not he or she is moving.

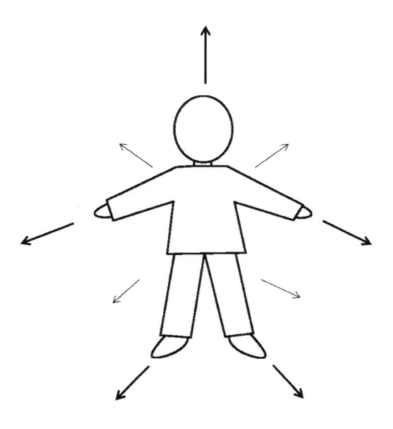

Journal Prompt: What would it look like for you to be still, but with energy flow "on"?

Try this. Stand up and extend your arms out. Try to switch the energy "on" and "off" while keeping your arms out to the sides. Can you feel a difference? Try to send energy from your back muscles through your arms and out of your finger tips. Does it look or feel any different?

ENGAGEMENT

The powerhouse of a dancer comes from the abdominal region, or the trunk of the body. Most of our movements, although we do not realize it, stem from that powerhouse. Other words used to describe this region of the body are "core" or "center". When energy is flowing through the core of the dancer, and the brain is sending signals to the core so that the movements of all other limbs originate from that core energy flow, that is *engagement.*

Not all dancers know how to properly engage their center of energy and direct all of their movements from there. It is certain that if one learns correct alignment and engagement, it will be much easier to learn and execute any dance phrase, step, or exercise. Engagement adds a professional quality to a dancer, whether they are just walking across a stage or doing twenty pirouettes! Anyone can move their limbs around, but not just anyone can move their whole body as a unit with precision and control stemming from their core.

PRACTICE, PRACTICE, PRACTICE!

Engagement and alignment do not come instantaneously. It takes constant practice, as with the mastering of any skill. It is a bit of an abstract concept, but do not fear! There are a few simple ways to practice engagement and condition the body to engage in a constant flow of energy from one's center.

NOTE: Through all of the following exercises, make sure to *BREATHE* and not to clench anything, but allow oxygen to flow into all of your muscles; In through the nose, and out through the mouth.

- Picture a string connected to the top of your head. (Not your forehead, but right at the center of the top of your head) This string connects to your spine and is constantly pulling you up. (Don't raise your shoulders, as this may be a common reaction to this imagery.) This causes a space in your core between the bottom of your ribs and the top of your pelvis, and a sense of liftedness. Remember this image as you dance.
- Stand up in proper alignment. Picture a string tied to your belly button and that someone was tugging that string towards your spine. Do not simply suck in your stomach, but try to engage the abdominal muscles underneath. Don't hold your breath! Relax your shoulders!
- Lay down on the floor, face up. Bend your legs so that the bottoms of your feet are on the floor in parallel position and your knees are bent. Put both hands in a triangle shape over your belly button and press down. Those are the right muscles to use. Try sucking those muscles in without using your hands. Then, let your knees start to fall to one side but catch them before their momentum takes them to the floor and center them again. Try to do that by using your abs to stop your legs instead of using your thigh muscles.

(Make sure the movement of your legs is very slight. Stop them almost as soon as they start moving.) That is what engagement is supposed to feel like when standing.

WEIGHT DISTRIBUTION

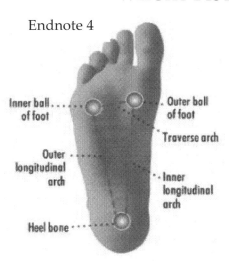

Endnote 4

Unless you're doing a handstand or some other type of acrobatic trick, your weight is always all on your feet. It has always been so amazing to me that our feet can handle so much weight all of the time! God designed our feet to hold weight in specific areas of the foot. It is interesting to realize that weight and where you distribute it actually greatly affects your dancing. Weight distribution can restrict or enable your movement. In Modern dance, body weight should be evenly distributed between the three main points of the foot. These main points are the inner ball, the outer ball, and the heel.

Although a dancer should always feel engaged and lifted, it is also necessary to feel grounded. Being "grounded" is when the dancer uses the floor's absorption to support and distribute his or her weight, rather than being lifted up out of the floor. A picture one can imagine to practice being grounded is the roots of a tree and how they dig into the floor. This isn't the same as being heavy into the floor or letting your weight sit on your bones, but rather it is about the way the energy flows. One's energy from the bottom limbs should drive into the floor, from the center down. And from the center up, one should feel lifted.

OPOSITION

You may ask yourself, "How am I supposed to be lifted but grounded at the same time? Those sound like opposites!" But that's exactly it! If a dancer learns to understand and acquire opposition, they can grow exponentially. Opposition may sound like something negative, but in the world of dance, it is actually a key element that one can use to be better grounded and to extend through a full range of motion.

Opposition is when different energy streams in the body go in different directions. If you look back to the image of the body with the arrows going out from it, you may see that some of the arrows are going in completely opposite directions.

Opposition can help with balance. To achieve good balance, the energy must stem from the core. From the belly button up there is a lifted feeling, and from the belly button down one feels the energy going into the floor. This is the essence of opposition. Instead of containing the energy or sending it all in one direction, the outspread manner in which one directs the energy adds class and balance to the performance quality of the dancer. It also makes everything much easier!

Journal Prompt: Spend some time discovering with your body what opposition feels like. Opposition can be found in many different areas and motions. Stretching your arms out to the sides can be a simple "statue" action, or it can be an action of opposition! Energy is being sent out from your core and back, through your arms, and out of your fingers in opposing directions!

ENDNOTES

1. *Ballerina Body*, Misty Copeland, p.34
2. http://humananatomylesson.com/muscle-of-the-lower-back/
3. https://anatomyclass123.com
4. http://www.anatomychartee.us/tag/nerves-in-human-body-length/
5. https://risadoren.wordpress.com

WARM YET? 2

> "A muscle is like a car. If you want it to run well early in the morning, you have to warm it up."
> — Florence Griffith Joyner

Before beginning a dance rehearsal or performance, a *pre*-warm-up is ideal. A dancer usually does this before class begins, but it is always refreshing to have a class where an instructor gives a set pre-warm-up. The purpose of a pre-warm-up is to prepare and relax the body for the movement it is about to execute. It also prepares the mind to learn and opens the pathways between the brain and the body. It's a time in which one can concentrate on one's own body and what it is feeling, mentally go over corrections or the elimination of certain habits, and center the body through breathing, waking up the joints, and practicing engagement.

It is important to note that dancing is not only about the body and how much we train it, but it is also largely about the *brain* and how we can train our brains to communicate with our bones and muscles to execute specific

movements—no matter how basic or complex. Brain training takes just as long or even longer to do than training the body; because we usually have to override pathways of "brain messages" to our bodies that have become muscle memory. A pre-warm-up helps with centering your body and focusing your brain! I love praying over my body as a pre-warm-up, and to remember to *speak life* over myself instead of focusing on the negatives. For example:
"Thank you God, for giving me legs that will walk and dance to places to show off your glory!"

Here are a few examples of exercises that can be included in a pre-warm-up:
1. Rolling up and rolling down the spine from a standing position
2. Rolling the ankles, neck, shoulders, and wrists
3. Engagement exercises
4. Using a foam roller on sore muscles or tender spots
5. Physically and mentally going over the correction of bad habits in a relaxed and positive manner
6. Even breathing

WARM-UP

After a pre-warm-up and before dancing fully, it is necessary to warm up the body. Our bodies are somewhat like plastic. When they are warm, they bend, and when they are cold, they tend to break! Having an elevated body temperature allows for the elasticity of the muscles, and therefore prevents injuries and improves flexibility. Injury prevention is the main reason for a warm-up, but it also prevents soreness after dancing! I've gone into rehearsals without warming up and woken up feeling like a truck ran over me the next morning. I've also injured myself by dancing without warming up. Warm-ups are also the perfect time to practice alignment and for strengthening the muscles. Here are some simple warm up exercises. For your most successful warm-up, keep them in this order:

1. Joints
   - Toes and ankles:

Roll your ankles while sitting or standing on one foot. Point through your toes or trot in place.

   - Hips

Hold onto the barre or a wall and swing one leg at a time to the front and back with your knee bent. This causes motion in your hip socket, warming it up.

Lay on your side with your legs bent. The leg on top should swing from behind you towards your chest. Initiate motion using your pelvis. Do it on the other side. Repeat.

   - Shoulders

Roll your shoulders forward and backwards and raise them up and down.

2. Spine and neck
   - Look left and right, up and down, and tilt right

and left with your head. Repeat in any sequence. Be careful not to "break" your neck, which means letting it hang back all the way because it can hurt your vertebrae.
- Put your hands on your hips and stand with your feet apart. Push your rib cage forward, right, back, and left. Repeat. Then move it in a circular motion. Switch directions.
- Move your hips side to side. Tuck and arch your pelvis.

3. Feet
    - Extending through the feet in simple and repetitive sequences whether sitting on the floor or standing.

4. Larger muscles
    - Legs: Jumping Jacks or trotting/jogging.
    - Arms: Rotate your arms in their sockets. Do some push ups!
    - Abdominals: Crunches or plank

5. Small jumps/ prancing/ skipping
    - A great way to warm up the lower extremities. Jump in place in sets of 8 or 16. Don't forget to fully extend through your feet in the air!

If you work with children or non-dancers, this is a fun and

efficient game to warm up the body with:

> From the toes all the way up to the head, try to isolate the body parts and explore by moving them in ways you never have before. Have one particular body part "lead" your movement all around the room. (I like to do toes, knees, hips, ribs, shoulders, elbows, wrists, fingers, and head. Sometimes I include nose, chin, and fun things like that!)

An important note is that this game does not guarantee a full warm-up; it is most usually used as a precursor or pre-warm-up. But, if the dancers just keep moving, they are bound to be very warm!

Another easy way to warm up is to make sure that the temperature of the room you are in isn't too cold. Although it may feel nice to be in a cold room when you are sweating, your muscles will not appreciate it!

Different bodies get warm in different ways. Some people naturally stay warmer for longer, and some people cool down quickly. I am in the latter group. This means that when I dance, I always have to have a sweater or socks with me. Wearing warm clothes helps me when I'm warming up, and putting them on when I am already warm helps me to stay warm. It also takes every person a different amount of time to warm up certain areas of the body.

Journal Prompt: Once you get to know your body, you can find out what body parts take longer to warm up for you. That way, you can pay a little more attention to those parts during your pre-warm-up, or make sure you are working to warm up those stubborn areas during warm-up.

3
"TECHNICALLY..."

Technique - *n*: the manner in which details are treated (as by a writer) or basic physical movements are used (as by a dancer) the ability to use such movements

— Merriam Webster Dictionary

There are many different dance techniques out there. Normally dancers will advocate for the technique that they practice. That's not a bad thing! Still, I'd like it to be clear that I am not using this book to advocate for a specific technique, but rather for the technical training of a dancer in general. I love Modern dance and have grown inmensly because of it. Improvisation and non-traditional movement are my forte. Whatever the technique is you would choose to study, the learning of that technique, the practice, the discipline, the effort, and the art—those I advocate for.

Most of what I share in this book I wrote down because I believe it can be easily picked up by anyone; even if you are that person who has always been told you cannot dance. Movement is for everyone. Learning through technique is just the way to protect our bodies and train ourselves to follow a specific practice.

Technique is skill or ability in a particular field; the field this book focuses on being dance. As mentioned earlier, technique helps to prevent injury. It may sound strange, but it makes sense! Basic dance technique is made in a way so that you can look beautiful but also care for your body at the same time. For example, pointing feet isn't just "pretty", but it helps with shock absorption when landing from a jump! Technical training also helps to more clearly communicate a message to the audience. Frankly, it looks better and clearer when a dancer is technically trained, because they have learned that "language" and can use it to speak to others. There is also a wider range of possibilities in movement when a dancer is technically trained, because they have explored more possibilities. I believe that every dancer who is part of a group or ministry should at least learn basic dance technique because it demonstrates that you can perform your craft with excellence and confidence. Although we are to understand that the heart is the most important part of dancing for the Lord, whether in or outside of the church, technique is also very crucial—especially if you feel called to be a dancer in the marketplace.

Technical training should first and foremost be given in a classroom setting. I cannot expect that you will read this book and automatically know how to execute a technical step properly. However, I still found it important to share some basic technique with my readers; especially those who have never had any technical training and want to assess themselves and apply basic technical corrections to their movement. Below are some descriptions of basic technical practices:

1. Pointing (or extending through the foot)
    - As soon as the feet leave the floor, they must always point and stay pointed until they come back to the floor, unless otherwise instructed by a choreographer or teacher.
    - Breaking this down: First the foot is in a ¾ point (heel off the ground), then in demi point (toes are left on the ground), and finally full point (only the top tip of the big toe is touching the floor or not at all)
    - Don't just crunch your toes. Make sure the top of the foot is fully stretched out when pointing.
    - Extending through the foot is especially important when jumping and landing. Landing through the foot is the opposite of extending, in which the foot touches the floor in the order of toe first, then the ball of the foot on the foor, and then the heel last.
    - Prancing is a simple exercise to practice extending fully through the foot. Once the ¾, demi, and full progression is understood and learned, repeat those steps seamlessly and alternate feet. Press down on the floor hard enough that it becomes a type of trot (called a "prance" in Modern Dance).
2. Turn out and parallel
    - Turn out explained: A "turned out" position is defined by the rotation of the hip sockets and where the knees and feet are placed due to that rotation. Dance movements can be done turned out—meaning that the each femur rotates

away from the center of the body from the hip socket by using the inner thigh and glutes. If the dancer is facing forward in a turned out position, the knees are pointing to the external sides of the dancer.

- Parallel explained: A "parallel" position is also defined by the rotation of the hips. The outcome of that rotation is that the toes and knees are pointing forward and the feet are parallel to each other. If the dancer is facing forward in parallel, the knees point forward.

- In Ballet, dancers always have turned out legs. In Modern, dancers switch from using turned out and parallel positions.

3. Arms and Hands

    - Arms: Energy should stem from the lats (latissimus dorsi) all the way through the finger tips. When arms are held to the sides, elbows should never sink in towards each other but be rotated away from each other. The shoulders should be pressed down and although there is energy flowing through the arms, there should be no tension.

    - Hands: Energy, not stiffness, in the fingers. Hands should not be gripping and neither should they be drooping. Placement of the fingers: Fingers extended fully and close to each other. The thumb is either close to the palm or tucked in towards the palm; never sticking up unless instructed. The pointer finger can float away from the other fingers slightly, not in towards the palm, but away from it.

    - When focusing too much on the lower extremities, a dancer can forget to shape the arms. The arms should always have volume and extend even past what the dancer feels is comfortable to them. Long lines are better than short lines.

4. Turns

- Spotting: While executing any turn, a dancer must spot to be able to locomote in the proper direction and to prevent dizziness and therefore be able to do more turns without falling. Most easily explained, the dancer keeps their head upright and looking in one direction while their body begins to rotate, right before completing a full rotation and when the neck can no longer twist, the dancer rapidly turns the head all the way around to look back at the same spot they were looking at before. This is all done before their body finishes the rotation. Spotting is best practiced in slow motion looking at oneself in the mirror just shimmying the feet around without focusing on any technical turn.

- Chaine Turns: (pronounced sheh-nay) Traveling turns that keep both legs extended and use both feet to locomote. It is derived from the French word for chain because many of these turns can be chained together. The movement is basically a "step together" repeated over and over again on the balls of the feet. The leading foot, or the one that steps first, determines the direction of the turn along with spotting. The turnout of the legs is what causes the rotation of the entire body once the second leg closes in. The dancer rotates around the shoulder above the leading leg. So, if my right leg leads, I turn towards my right shoulder.

- Pirouettes: Can be done turned out and turned in. They are most usually started from a fourth position, where the feet are separated from each other, one in front and one behind. The dancer bends their knees and springs up onto one leg while the other leg bends and the toe attaches to the inside of the supporting leg, touching the knee. The spin can happen in either direction. This turn does not travel.

BARRERA

4
ELASTI-GIRL

"Success is due to our stretching to the challenges of life. Failure comes when we shrink from them."
— John C. Maxwell

Flexibility doesn't just look cool, it is also makes different movements easier, less straining on the body, and more fluid. Being flexible also prevents injury and it maximizes the movement vocabulary of a dancer. Flexibility is not attained overnight; it takes commitment and constant stretching. Some people are more naturally flexible than others. If you are one of those people, praise God, because becoming flexible isn't easy!

Praying when you stretch and speaking positively to your muscles and joints is something I learned truly helps in this long and arduous process. It is important to be kind to our body and to speak life into it![1] Speaking over your body is also a great exercise to run with your dance ministry team, for example. It unifies the dancers in prayer over their own bodies, but adds that spiritual dimension that we otherwise go without!

Three CRUCIAL things to know before embarking on the journey to flexibility:
1. Be warm when you stretch to gain flexibility. It is very possible to pull a muscle if you stretch when your body is cold. The warmer you are, the better you stretch!!
2. BREATHE through everything. Clenching muscles is our bodies' natural reaction to pain, but unfortunately it will not help at all when trying to get more flexible. Relax. Relaxing does not mean letting your guts hang out; still suck in your abs!
3. Do not push yourself past your limit. If you are experiencing a sharp or stinging type of pain, or you feel it is too much to handle, STOP or lessen the intensity of the stretch.

DYNAMIC VS. STATIC STRETCHING

When most people think of stretching, they picture a ballerina getting squashed down into a painful split by her Russian instructor. (Okay maybe that's just me!) Your image of stretching is probably not so extreme, but it is most likely a static stretch you are envisioning. A static stretch is when one stretches a part of the body by holding the muscles in a certain place and not moving for a set amount of time. Although this is the most common understanding of what stretching is, this is not the only way!

Dynamic stretching is when a dancer or mover begins to develop elasticity through a movement that stretches the limits of his or her muscles. An example of a dynamic stretch can be a big kick (grande battement) with an extended leg. This repeated motion can actually improve the flexibility of a dancer. It must obviously be done when warm, but it is a very effective and dare I say more fun way to develop flexibility. This type of stretching is actually healthier and easier on the body than static stretching. I, however, endorse both; only if the static stretching is done properly.

To be successful, each of the following stretching exercises should be held for at least 30 seconds each and practiced every other day. I personally would recommend holding each stretch for a minute every day. Do not stay in stretches for longer than three minutes each. Static stretching is not good for you if it is done for long periods of time.

1. Lunge
    - In a deep lunge, (leg extended directly behind) make sure the bent knee is directly above the heel. The back leg should be fully extended and the palms of your hands should be on the floor by your foot.
    - In a deep lunge, (leg to the side) your knee should point towards the ceiling and your hands should be on the floor in front of you. Flex and point foot of the extended leg.
2. Butterfly and Frog (Hip rotation):
    - Butterfly: Sit on the floor and put the bottoms of the feet together. Try to open your legs as far as possible. Bend over and touch your nose to your

toes. Don't forget to keep thinking about your belly button being pulled towards your spine.
- Frog: Lie on your stomach with your legs in a diamond (bottoms of the feet together). Try to let your feet drop towards the floor as much as possible, keeping your pelvis on the ground. Don't worry if your feet don't touch the floor, just let them hang.

3. Back/ abdomen:
   - Back/ abs stretch: Lie on your stomach, put your palms on the floor right under your shoulders and press up until your arms are straight and the lower half of your body stays on the ground. Keep your shoulders down.
   - Hold onto a barre or a partner. Put your feet in a parallel position, hip width apart. Pull away from the barre, bend your knees, and tilt your pelvis back (tuck it under) while curving your head and neck down. The pulling away causes a stretching of the back muscles.

4. Feet:
   - Sit on the floor Indian style. Lift up one foot using your hand (right hand to right foot), grabbing underneath the ankle. Without sickling your foot, use your other hand to press down on the top of your arch while you point your foot. Pull your toes towards you.
   - With a partner, extend your legs out in front of you while sitting on the floor. Point your feet.

Partner uses their hands to press your point down from the top of your arch in a pull and press motion.
5. Hamstrings:
   - Sit on the floor Indian style. Extend one of your legs. Reach for your foot with a pointed foot and then flexed.
   - Extend both legs towards the front while sitting on the floor. Reach up with your arms and then over towards your toes. Repeat with flexed feet. The goal is to bend your torso over onto your legs so that they touch, while holding onto your feet, with the top of your head pointing towards the front. Keep your knees straight.
6. Calves:
   - Find a wall or a barre. Hold onto the wall and take one large step back with one leg. Bend the front knee. Keep your hands on the wall and your torso upright while pressing your heel into the ground and keeping the back leg straight.
7. Quads:
   - While standing, pick up one leg behind you by grabbing your ankle and try to touch the bottom of your foot to your bottom. Remember to engage. Try to keep your knees together.
8. Split
   - Right and Left splits should be done with turned out legs.
   - If splits are too difficult, sit on one knee as it is

bent and extend the other leg towards the front and reach for your foot.
- Deep lunges help too. If a lunge has become easy, tuck the toes of the back leg and rest the back knee on the ground. Allow the pelvis to drop further towards the ground, so it stretches out the groin and psoas. You can also turn out your front leg and put your elbows on the ground by the inside of your leg.

9. Straddle
   - Sitting on the floor, open legs to the sides. With flexed feet, toes should be pointing towards the ceiling, not the floor. Stretch to the sides reaching for your feet. Bend your torso forward and extend your arms forward on the floor. The goal is to get your stomach flat on the floor while your knees still point towards the ceiling. Do NOT let your knees turn in and point anywhere other than up. Repeat with point and flexed feet.

Journal Entry: Try to track your flexibility over a set period of time and record it by writing it down or taking pictures.

DRAW A PARALLEL:

Just like when we have to stretch to get more flexible, the Lord stretches us constantly in our faith walks. He asks us to do things that are scary or painful; He allows moments that seem painful without reason. Perhaps He leads you to a job you are uncomfortable in, or to confront a friend about a touchy issue. In the natural, you can react to stretching by getting stiff and resisting, but that's going to get you no where. Stretching is painful, but it is good for us because it helps with injury prevention and aesthetic. Spiritual stretching is the same way. We can resist a stretching from the Lord, but it will get us no where. Instead, we have to breathe in the oxygen of the Holy Spirit and go with it. Lean into the stretch and understand that although it is painful, it will help with preventing injury in the future, and help you to reach new heights!

ENDNOTES

1. Proverbs 18: 21

5
CONDITIONING

"It is because the body is a machine that education is possible. Education is the formation of habits, a super inducing of an artificial organization upon the natural organization of the body."

— Thomas Henry Huxley

"The LORD is my strength and my shield; my heart trusts in him, and he helps me. My heart leaps for joy, and with my song I praise him."

— Psalm 28:7

I have seen dancers that are very flexible, but lack strength. This can be a problem because they don't have the ability to hold anything extended for long, and their coordination is lessened due to this lack of strength. Just like flexibility, strength building (or conditioning) is also a process. Conditioning is a process to develop muscles the way dancers need them. We need strength in order to jump higher, dance for longer periods of time, to hold our bodies and limbs better, and to lift other dancers, too!

Some of these excercises might seem difficult at first, or it may even seem like you aren't very good at doing them. My advice is to keep going. At first, even if you can't do one push up, don't give up! When I first started doing real push ups, I couldn't get myself up off of the ground for a second push up! It took me three weeks of slowly lowering myself down and trying a single push up until I was able to do it! Like I said, it really is a process and it takes dedication to learn and get stronger. Don't be discouraged if you start with smaller sets, because if you stick at it, you will get stronger before you know it!

The first way to develop a strong body is to dance and dance often. That's the easy one. There are different conditioning excercises that keep your body fit for dancing. Strength building for dancers is actually different than strength building for non-dancers. For dancers, conditioning is paired with stretching to help develop long, lean, muscles. Remember, dancers need to have long and strong muscles, not short and bulky ones! So, when you do these conditioning exercises, stretch out the muscles you use once you're done.

- Core strengthening
    - Crunches: Lay down with your back on the floor. Plant your feet on the floor hip-width apart in a parallel position. Clasp your hands behind your lift your shoulder blades off the floor by using your abdominal muscles. Make sure to keep your

elbows opened wide. Keep your neck lengthened. (Remember, belly button to the spine!) Do in sets of 20. Repeat as many times as needed.

- o Lower abs: lay flat on the ground face up. Lift both of your legs while keeping them together and straight with the toes pointed. Lower them down until they are about 6 inches from the floor, and lift them up again. Keep your spine pressed into the floor (the tendency is to arch). Repeat as needed. (For an extra challenge, repeat the motion while criss-crossing your legs)

- o Planks: (type 1) In a push up position, your weight is distributed evenly between your hands and the balls of your feet. Your body should be kept in a straight line from the tip of your head to your feet. Don't forget to engage your core. Hold this position for 30 seconds or more. (type 2) Similar to type 1 except your weight is distributed between your forearms and the balls of your feet.

- Inner Thighs

  - o Lay on the floor on your right side. Bend your left leg and cross it in front of the extended leg. Plant the bottom of your left foot on the floor by your right knee. Plaace your left palm on the floor in front of your chest. Make sure your body is in a straight line from the top of your head to the bottoms of your feet. Lift your right leg up off the floor in small and quick reps (keep the leg extended). Switch between a pointed and flexed foot. Repeat on your left side!

- Glutes

- o Get on the floor on all fours. Make sure your spine is straight and your core is engaged. Extend one leg behind you in the air in a kicking motion. Do in reps of 5, 10, 15, or 20. Repeat with the other leg.

- o Start in the same position as the last exercise, but instead of kicking backwards; open your leg as it's still bent to the side. See that it reaches the height of your hips. Do in reps of 5, 10, 15, or 20. Repeat with the other leg.

- Arms

    - o Push ups: Get into a plank (type 1) and bend your elbows to lower your body without allowing your torso or legs to touch the floor. Keep your body straight (tendency is to lift up the hips). Push back up into a plank position. Repeat as needed.

    - o Sit on the floor comfortably. Extend your arms out to the sides and make small circles with your arms going forward for 16 counts. Change the direction of the circles and repeat for another 16 counts. Then, with your palms facing forward, do small presses forward for 16. Repeat with your palms facing the back. Repeat this routine as needed.

- Calves

    - o Releves: With feet together either in a parallel or turned out position; bend both knees and spring up onto the balls of your feet (demi pointe). Lower down to a flat foot and bent knees. Repeat as needed.

- - Eleves: With feet together either in a parallel or turned out position; from straight legs, rise up onto the balls of your feet (demi pointe). Lower down to a flat foot and straight legs. Repeat as needed.
- Back
  - Lay flat on the floor facedown. Clasp your hands behind your head. Open up your elbows wide. Keep your legs on the floor, and raise your torso up off of the ground (back will be arched). Lower back down to the floor. Repeat as needed. If you need help, ask a friend to hold your ankles down.
- Feet
  - Grab a towel or an old t-shirt and put it on the ground. Sit down and place your right foot on the towel. Spread your toes wide and try pulling it towards you by curling your toes. Repeat on both feet.

DRAW A PARALLEL

I could be technically proficient, fluid, and know dance terminology, but if I don't condition my body, I cannot execute movement to my full capacity. Strength is an obvious necessity in dance which is achieved through conditioning and practice.

In the parable of the sower, Jesus talks about the seed being planted among different soils. The seed sown on rocky soil is like the seed sown in a person who has not conditioned their character or their faith. "(yet)... he has no root in himself, but endures for a while, and when tribulation or persecution arises on account of the word, immediately he falls away" [1]

Our faith starts off as a small mustard seed[2]*. It has to be cultivated so it grows, just like when we condition our bodies. This cultivation of our faith and character happens through different experiences in our lives when the Lord calls us trust to Him through our obedience.*

Sometimes we can have a lot of knowledge, but we haven't developed enough character to put that knowledge into practice. When our roots haven't grown deep enough in our own idenitites in Christ, it is tough to conquer the oppositions in our lives. Conditioning our faith in the Lord and His word helps us to withstand the storms.[3]

ENDNOTES

1. Matthew 13:21
2. Luke 17:6
3. Matthew 7:24

BARRERA

6

NUTRITION
AND BODY CARE

"Life is like riding a bicycle. To keep your balance, you must keep moving."
— Albert Einstein

The body is the temple of the Holy Spirit. It amazes me every time I think about it to know that my body is the literal house of the Spirit of God. I have a responsibility to then care for that temple, and so do you! This next section will share some guidelines on nutrition and health for anyone that seeks to maintain his or her body in a healthy balance.

FOOD

Aside from drinking enough water, eating properly is probably the most important way to take care of your body. Basic healthy eating requires a protein-filled diet, vitamins, nutrients, the proper carbohydrates, and the right amount of food at the right time. It sounds like a long list, but truly there are some very practical steps to a healthy diet. Sugars and processed foods should be avoided in their totality; which is probably the most difficult part! I like to allow two days or three where I can actually eat dessert in the week, but finding healthy alternatives for sugary desserts is something that you could try if you're a big sweet tooth. Protein is especially important to one's diet. Chicken, beef, fish, and different grains are all protein rich. Taking supplements is also a great way to get the different vitamins and minerals you need, as well as eating plenty of vegetables and fruits. Carbs can also be good for you, if you eat the right kind of carbs, such as whole-wheat pasta and bread, oatmeal, barley, acorn squash, black beans, sweet potatoes, legumes, and quinoa. Even fat is good for you.

"One of the greatest secrets I have learned over the course of my career is that fat—eating it, absorbing it, and burning it for energy—is key to building the muscle and providing the strength so important... to perform at such a high level for hours, day in and day out."[3]

Here Copeland is referring to fats that are actually beneficial for your body, such as fish, nuts, and avocados. Finally, it isn't just about what you eat but about how many times you eat. It is better for the body to receive small meals more frequently than fewer large meals spread out during the day. This increases your metabolism.

Metabolism: noun - the sum of the processes in the buildup and destruction of **protoplasm**; SPECIFICALLY : the chemical changes in living cells by which energy is provided for vital processes and activities and new material is assimilated[1]

Basically this definition of metabolism tells us that different chemical changes in the body cause us to have energy. When those chemical processes occur more easily and more quickly, that is a fast metabolism. To keep your metabolism where it should be, you should not over-eat. You should eat enough to be satisfied, but not to where you are *so* full. A good way to tell whether or not you're actually hungry is to know if you are properly hydrated. Often times we feel hungry when what we actually need is water.

DRAW A PARALLEL

The word is our daily bread.[2] Just as our metabolism speeds up when we eat often and eat properly, we can increase our "spiritual metabolism". If we constantly eat from the Lord's word, we can learn to digest and pull energy from His word better and faster as we grow. It sounds simple, but it is very true. If you eat the word daily, you actually have more energy to fight off different attacks and spiritual diseases. If you eat the word constantly, you acquire an understanding of the language of Heaven, process it adequately, and take in more nutrients from it than your first few times tasting it. The word never goes stale!

HYDRATION

Before discussing hydration, I'd like to discuss the effects of dehydration. I know that I often did not take drinking water seriously, until I realized that it was the major cause in most of my bodily problems. As astonishing as it may sound, dehydration actually causes a large variety of mishaps in the human body; that is because two thirds of our bodies are made up of water! Dehydration can cause muscle cramps, weakness and shakiness, headaches, bad breath, dry skin, and feelings of hunger, to mention just a few! Dehydration causes so many ailments in our body![4]

Many of us have heard that to stay hydrated, you must drink 8 glasses of water a day. More recently I learned that there is a way to calculate the amount of water you need based on the amount of exercise you do daily and your body weight. "...your body uses water to maintain its temperature, remove waste, and lubricate joints. Water is needed for good health."[5]

DRAW A PARALLEL

His presence is our hydration.[6] It seems so simple, but it is actually something that many people miss. After dancing, I'm thirsty. My initial reaction is to grab my water bottle. Sometimes I feel like drinking something bad for me, like a Coke. But I know in the end a Coke won't hydrate me. Nothing is better than water to quench thirst. We do the same thing in our lives so many times. We go through something, whether good or bad, in our lives and we get thirsty. Instead of turning to our Source, which is the Holy Spirit and His presence, we turn to other things. We grab our "Coke" for hydration: the T.V., a friend to gossip to, that vice, or that thing that will temporarily satisfy our thirst. Jesus is the only true Source that satisfies our souls. Aside from satisfying us, keeping ourselves physically hydrated prevents the many ills of dehydration in our bodies. It is the same spiritually!

"*Dehydration can cause muscle cramps, weakness and shakiness, headaches, bad breath, dry skin, and feelings of hunger*". **I can think of a spiritual application for each one of those: Muscle cramps are weaknesses in character. Weakness is weakness in the flesh. Shakiness is not being built on the rock. Headaches are opening our minds to attacks and lies of the enemy. Bad breath is a reflection of a bad heart, which is revealed by negative words. Dry skin is being constantly or easily irritated. Feelings of hunger are an awakening in your flesh for sin. Those are some terrible effects of spiritual dehydration!! Let's do ourselves and everyone around us a favor and stay hydrated in the presence of Jesus!**

SLEEP

I am really bad at this one. Thank God I have been getting better, but especially a few years ago I had no self control to get to bed on time. It is very obvious that human beings need sleep to function. If a baby is cranky, they are usually just tired. The same things happen to us as adults. Of course, there are health risks other than crankiness that a lack of sleep causes. When we don't sleep, we have a greater risk of becoming depressed and anxious. Not sleeping can impair your memory; so as a dancer we definitely need our sleep to remember all of the steps in choreography! Your immune system is strengthened through sleep. Gaining weight can also be a direct consequence of a lack of sleep.[7] We are also more likely to cause accidents and injure ourselves and even others when we do not sleep enough. As dancers and servants of God, we have to steward our time and sleep well, so that we can stay sharp and aware of our surroundings, both physical and spiritual.

I have also noticed in my own experience that when I am tired I am also more vulnerable to spiritual attack. My emotions get harder to handle, and I can easily start slipping into thoughts that aren't from God. I think this is because the energy I have left is being spent trying to stay awake and do normal things, taking away from the energy I could place into self assessment and intercession throughout the day. It's true that we should be disciplined enough to wake up early in the morning to pray and spend time with the Lord, but that also means we should be disciplined enough to steward our time so that we get enough sleep to do those things. Sometimes that means not watching that last episode on Netflix that I really want to watch, or putting my phone down and understanding that Facebook and Instagram will still be there tomorrow!

FIRST PRAYER, THEN RICE!

Although as dancers we try our best not to get injured, unfortunately, it still happens sometimes. When you do get injured, there is a proper way to take care of an injury so that you heal up quickly and can regain the strength you need in that area so the injury doesn't repeat itself.

First, prayer. When we hurt ourselves, we often go to the worst case scenario in our minds: "How bad is it? *Oh no.* Will I be able to dance? *Oh NO!*" It goes somewhat in a downward spiral after that! It's important to train ourselves to address the Lord instead of our own minds when we get injured. Instead of having an inner monologue of how much it hurts and how bad it is, try changing it to an inner dialogue. Pray. Ask Jesus to come and heal instantly. Take a second to remember that God is sovereign and to surrender your body to Him once more. It hurts, but it is worth it to pray first. I am a firm believer that God can heal supernaturally. I also believe that He can use doctors and medicine to heal people, too. Either way, no matter the route you take, still pray!

After prayer, comes R.I.C.E., which stands for:

Rest

Ice

Compression

Elevation

This is a dancers go-to method for an injured body member. Resting is the first component of the R.I.C.E. method. It's hard not to move around when you are a natural born mover, but you have to rest from using the injured part of your body. Ice reduces inflammation and should be applied 2 or 3 times a day in intervals of 15-20 minutes. "Compression will also be used during the recovery process in the forms of bandages, supports and tape; this will further reduce swelling and help to protect the area from further injury... The most significant effect of compression is to reduce internal bleeding in the soft tissue surrounding the injury."[8]

Lastly comes elevation. Elevation applies only when you can actually elevate the injured body part, for example a knee, foot, or wrist. Elevation decreases the pressure of the blood in the area of the trauma. This also allows for inflammation to decrease and for healing to happen more quickly.

ENDNOTES

1. Merriam Webster's Dictionary
2. Matthew 4:4
3. *Ballerina Body* – Misty Copeland – p.
4. "What Happens to Your Body When You're Dehydrated"
   – http://articles.mercola.com/dehydration-symptoms.aspx
5. "Hydration: Why its so Important"
   – http://familydoctor.org
6. John 4:14
7. "Get Enough Sleep"
   –http://www.mentalhealthamerica.net
8. "Compression – Sports Injury Treatment"
   – http://www.nsmi.org.uk

SECTION THREE

ON EARTH
AS IN HEAVEN

Truly I say to you, **whatever you loose on earth will be loosed in Heaven, and whatever you bind on earth shall be bound in Heaven.**
—Matthew 18:18

...your kingdom come, your will be done, **on earth as it is in heaven.**
—Matthew 6:10

DANCE OF LOVE

As I was writing Heaven Moves, Jesus changed things up on me. I originally intended for this book to be no more than a 60 page guide on how to treat your body well and develop intimacy with Jesus. What I didn't know was that the Lord was going to start to whisper to me the message He wants to share with His Bride. It took me two years to complete this book for that very reason. As soon as I thought that I was close to being done, Jesus gave me a new section to write. He kept on burdening me with this message: "My beloved, will you dance with me??" It is a question for the individual reading this book. Jesus is asking you if you are willing to trust Him with your life. He is asking that you would take His hand and let Him lead you and guide all of your steps. This question is for you in your own relationship with the Lord, but it is also for the Church. He is asking through His very Spirit: *My bride, will you move with me? One day I will return and we will dance to our wedding song. Follow my lead?*

He loves you. He wants you to trust Him fully, because anything that you could ever dream of is surpassed by His dreams for you. When you choose to trust Him and let Him lead your movement, He has the open channel to pour out His love over you. Jesus wildly rejoices when we follow His prompting. He is seeking those who will obey Him from the heart, out of faith and trust, in spirit and in truth. He isn't a control freak or a manipulator; He wants us to say yes to Him because He loves us.

THE CHURCH BODY

In 1 Corinthians 12:12-27, Paul speaks of the Church having different members, like a body, and Christ being the head of those members. This passage is special to me because I am a dancer and I love learning about my body. In this case, I get an inside look at the Church Body and how it works. I was so very glad to learn that Paul used the image of a body to describe the Church, because I was able to understand it in a different dimension, since I often study the body and love finding parallels between dance and our spiritual lives. In his letter he urges the church members to act like members of one body—functioning in unity with one another. Verses fourteen through twenty refer to every individual having a specific function, while all still being considered part of the same body; then Pual addresses division and unity in verses twenty-one through twenty-seven.

When I picture the Church as a large body, I often picture the body of a woman. I do this because the Church is the Bride of Christ. So, I often imagine a woman that stands over the earth. I start to picture what it would look like as a dancer if my body parts were not cooperating with one another, and I translate that mental image onto the Church; its' organs/members moving in opposing directions at times, and with very different goals in mind. It's almost like a body self-destructing when its immune system believes there is an infection and starts to shut down the organs. The Church, unfortunately, sometimes seems like a dysfunctional body; we do not get along, slander other members of the church, or think we are better than the person next to us. I feel that we have allowed many things to enter the Body and to disease it; whether it be outer attacks of the enemy or, more commonly, our own egos.

Take a person with paralysis as another example. In a case of parapledia, for instance, a person does not receive signals from their brain that tells their legs to move. I consider that in our case Jesus is the head or the Body. Jesus, the brain, is trying to tell us to move somewhere but we simply do not respond! That can be an example of pride or fear getting in the way of the movement of the Lord and what He wants to do. The issue of alignment, then, becomes a very important one! When each member is aligned, (just as when we align our spines, hips, knees, and the rest) the Body is able to move in fluidity with its partner—the Holy Spirit. It is the image of a healthy Body. This alignment has global impact because the Church is a Body that expands all over the world. Imagine the effect your alignment as an indivual has. Then add your brother's alignment to that. Then multiply it by your congregation's alignment, and the congregation down the street, and then every other congregation on the earth! The impact would be profound.

We as dancers often hear the phrase "be nice to your body" which means, feed it properly, sleep enough, don't overdo it, and especially don't allow negative self talk or self image enter your mind. I challenge you to apply this phrase to the the Church Body. Check yourself: If you are being "nice to your body" you cannot say bad things about it. You cannot insult your brother or sister, another denomination, or the church around the corner. If you are to be healthy, beautiful, and functioning, you must treat your body (our body) right! Working together with other members of the Body instead of allowing jealousy and pride to attack and take the lead is exactly what we need to do to be "nice to the body." It is time for us to put aside childish ways and grow up in our faith[1]; and see that the dream of God is to come back for *one* Bride in the end. I know and declare that we are starting to begin to see the entire Church Body being aligned to the movement of the Holy Spirit; functioning in unity and love; preparing herself for the coming of her groom.

THE UNVEILING

I believe that we are coming into an era where dance is being unveiled within the church. Historically dance has not mixed well with the Protestant faith; however Christians have begun to ask questions and break the boxes of traditions that were not biblical. Although dance is now miles ahead of where it was years ago, I can still (sadly) say that there is often still a great lack of professionality in the arts within the Church; especially in dance.

Many Christians have accepted one of two paradigms: Either dance and God do not combine or people should only dance for the Lord (and not the world). Neither of these are biblically accurate. The Word clearly says that we are not *of* the world, but we shine as lights *in* the world. Just as a doctor should not stop being a doctor simply because he is a Christian, a dancer should not stop performing just because they are Christian. They should be the light and use their art to bring Heaven to earth.

There is a revelatory wave of movement that is now sweeping across the nations. In the church, those who are learning about the grace, love, and freedom of the Spirit are also introducing dance into their church services. They are also letting dance out of the four walls. Dancers can now be missionaries and impart things such as healing and prophecy directly from the heavens while being in places of darkness—whether that is in big rich cities or poor rural areas.

Dance is starting to be unveiled in the church as the true light that it is. The Lord will use dance to bring healing to nations. Dance will attract sinners to the cross. The Bride of Christ will be a dancing bride, demonstrating freedom and joy for all those oppressed and imprisoned to see.

A MOVEMENT, NOT A MONUMENT

<u>Monument</u>: noun – a statue, building, or other structure erected to commemorate a famous or notable person or event.

Humanity must move to survive. Anything that is alive needs to move, no matter how hard it tries not to. Plants' microscopic cells swish around inside their stems. Animals run and hunt and play. Our lungs, our heart beat, our blood rushing through our veins – they are all indicators that we are alive. We breathe. We move. We live. I ask myself this question then: Why do others insist that the church body should remain motionless? Wouldn't that indicate that it is actually dead?

It is time to understand that the Church is not a monument. It is not a building erected to commemorate Jesus—it is a living organism that is supposed to move with Him as He leads. "The Spirit of God *moved* over the face of the waters" and He is moving over you today. He is brooding over you; incubating the life that He deposited inside of you. He made you for abundant life and for a great purpose. You don't even have to dance to truly move with Him! You can move with Him through any and all of the choices that you make. The Kingdom of God advances. I urge you to move forward with it. The time of being static is over. The Church can no longer be a memorial, as if Jesus had died and not returned to life. Jesus, the word, is alive and active [1]; and we are His extension! All living things are given life by the word or breath of God; and we who are alive cannot stop moving no matter what, lest we stiffen and die.

So, as the Church Body that called to awaken and partner with the movement of the Holy Spirit [2], how is it that we get ourselves moving? We must answer the question "What does movement look like for the Church of Christ?" and we must take the steps to fully understand and do it.

To move with the Holy Spirit, we need to align our beings. We need to actively love Him and spend time with Him in the secret place, where we get to know His heart. We should live a lifestyle where He is seated on the throne of our hearts. To further the accuracy of our alignment, we must treat our spirits, our souls, and our bodies properly; nourishing them in the ways they must be nourished. Our spirits must spend time with the Lord and with the Word. Our souls must be satisfied by the river of His presence which is the only true source of life. Our bodies must be rested and taken care of properly. The Church must also align itself. The Church must move, with Jesus as its Head (source) [3], and be the extension of His life. We must flow with the currents of the Holy Spirit, and not against them; together as a unit that is aligned to His moving. The Bride— she is being prepared to dance with her Bridegroom. She cannot be stiff. She cannot be unhealthy. She must yield to His leading hand that is gently placed on her back, and she must trust fully that He will not drop her or mislead her.

When I dance, I want to represent the Bride. I want to call her forth and say, "Hey, remember that you move only to His sweet leading. Remember that nothing else but the voice of your Lover causes your body to respond. Remember that you love Him more than anything else; and that He has a heart for the broken." We love the broken and the dying, and we move over them to spring forth life and life abundant.

"For in Him we live and move and have our being..."
(Acts 17:28)

ENDNOTES

1. Hebrews 4:12
2. Ephesians 5:14
3. Ephesians 5:23- The word *kephalē* (head) in this context — meaning *source* or *origin*.

BARRERA

JOURNAL

One great thing about journaling is that you can go back, review what you have learned, and track your own individual progress. No two journals look the same. Record what you have learned through reading "Heaven Moves" and write, draw, or paste pictures about your dance process!

Heaven Moves – Journal

Heaven Moves — Journal

BARRERA

Heaven Moves – Journal

BARRERA

Heaven Moves – Journal

ABOUT THE AUTHOR

Stephanie Barrera studied and graduated with a BA in Dance Pedagogy at Palm Beach Atlantic University in May 2015. Daughter to Michelle and Hernan Barrera, She was born in Barranquilla, Colombia and moved to the United States of America when she was just a baby, and her parents were missionaries called to the U.S. Learning both Spanish and English at an early age, Stephanie excelled in school and in the arts. She dedicated her life to the Lord from childhood, and served on her first missionary trip when she was fourteen. After that, she resolved to do everything she did for the cause of the Kingdom and travelled to Mexico, Brazil, Greece, Dominican Republic, Canada, Africa, and Colombia spreading the Love of Jesus.

In December 2016, she organized her first Dance Missions trip to Colombia with the company start-up she founded, Dancing Waters. The company is now in its second season and has recently completed their first summer program as well. *Heaven Moves* was in the process of being written during this time and it is her freshman publication, although she intends to continue writing.

Stephanie is also involved in other areas of the arts, such as painting and sculpting. She has also recorded and released several music singles and is working on a full length album.

"If you ask me what I'm passionate about, the first thing I'm going to tell you isn't dance, it isn't music, it isn't painting. It's loving. I can't imagine a life where we didn't have the purpose of loving God and loving people. That definitely would not be a life worth living. Every day I ask the Lord to show me more and more about how to love as He loves… through movement, art, a smile, or a word."

- Stephanie Barrera

Made in the USA
Columbia, SC
30 May 2018